# You Were Never Born

Also by John Wheeler

Awakening to the Natural State
Shining in Plain View
Right Here, Right Now

# You Were Never Born

John Wheeler

NON-DUALITY PRESS

NON-DUALITY PRESS
6 Folkestone Road  Salisbury SP2 8JP  United Kingdom
www.non-dualitybooks.com

Copyright © John Wheeler 2007

Cover design: John Gustard

With thanks to Leslie Caren for editorial assistance and proofreading

First Printing: April 2007

All rights reserved. No part of this publication may be reproduced or transmitted in any form or by any means, electronic or mechanical, including photocopying, recording or by any information or retrieval system without written permission by the publisher, except for the inclusion of brief quotations within a review.

ISBN 10: 0-9553999-2-0
ISBN 13: 978-0-9553999-2-3

# Preface

The first time I laid eyes on John Wheeler, I don't know what I was expecting, exactly, but that wasn't it. Perhaps from attending too many California satsangs and reading too many books written by spiritual celebrities, I was somehow expecting this guy to be just another guru clone, wafting into the room on a sense of his own specialness.

But I knew the moment I saw John that there was a clarity here I had not encountered in my twenty-five years on the spiritual scene. Here was a humble, working guy with no interest whatsoever in having me or anyone else look up to him, be in awe of him, or elevate him in any way. I saw a guy who knew his true nature, without a doubt in the world about it. I saw a guy who felt lucky to have ended his search a couple of years earlier by hearing what 'Sailor' Bob Adamson had to say, and now was moved, by love, to help others end their search as well.

John cut right to the chase, telling the folks gathered there at his book-signing at East West Bookstore in Mountain View, California, about his own twenty-year search and how it ended. We were riveted by him, by the candor with which he told his story. It struck me as a little odd that he didn't seem very interested in selling books. He held up his latest offering and waved it around a little bit, but mostly to illustrate to us that what we were looking for could not be found in there. And he went on, patiently, gently, and methodically, to tell us—show us—that what we had been looking for all these years was already so simply what we are, and what we experience as ourselves, right now. In that room, on that night, I finally understood.

I didn't mean to imply that John's books are unimportant—on the contrary, his writings are among the most valuable and most effective that exist on the subject of non-dualism. They are as effective as they are in large part because there is no confusion in John Wheeler. None. He got completely clear on this understanding in 2003, during a visit to Bob Adamson in Melbourne, Australia, and that was it.

No further doubts, no gray areas, no questions about the best and clearest way to communicate this, no sense of importance as the carrier of the message—none of these things has ever arisen for John. He is clear as a bell on the essential liberating points, and he doesn't stray from them. I've even heard John referred to as "relentless," which in some cases could be considered disparaging, but when it comes to the absolute—one without a second—a relentless approach is well-advised. It works for John—people seem to fall off the log quite often after meeting with him once or twice.

John has titled this, his fourth collection of dialogues and pointers, "You Were Never Born" which speaks to the very first principle: the fact that pure nothingness is all that exists, and that all of our personal problems and suffering are imaginary. John says, "You cannot speak of the birth of that which has no form or limits. We are that, and that has never come into form. So we have never been born." This simple truth is the bedrock underlying all the slippery layers of assumptions and projections that we try to heap on top of it. There is only the one truth, only the one principle, only the one which has no form or limits, and this is what you are. And that is the point to which John returns over and over again in his dialogues and pointers.

This is a great service, and rarer than we realize, because John does not muck up the truth with a lot of tangential ideas and mental diversions, as we find in so many other writings of this type. This clarity—this purity of focus—is the hallmark of John's teaching, and what makes him unique in this field.

In this, his latest book, this clarity is present, as usual, but in addition, there is a maturity that has been taking place in the means of communication. So I would not hesitate to say that this is John's best book yet.

John has a special place in my heart because he pointed out to me—and gave me the confidence to find for myself—that which I had been hungering for all my adult life. Let John speak to your heart, and you too may end your search now.

Annette Nibley
Mill Valley, California
October, 2006

## Table of Contents

*Preface by Annette Nibley*   v

The Basics
    Review of the Basics   3
    The Key Points   7
    Questions for Self-Knowledge   9
    Why Did Separation Ever Arise?   20
    Memory   22
    Ongoing Practice?   24
    Take the Focus Off of the Mind   26

Dialogues with John

1. Who Is Aware of Thought?   29
2. There Is No One Apart from This   31
3. Follow the Insights Back to Your Real Nature   34
4. This Is Easy and Effortless   37
5. Do Whatever Comes Up Next   40
6. Keep Things Simple   42
7. Pain and Suffering   45
8. Why Something Rather Than Nothing?   47
9. Awareness Is Not Knowable by the Mind   49
10. There Is No Need to Improve the Recognition   51
11. Handling Doubts and Confusion   54
12. Life Finds Its Natural Expression   55
13. There Is No One   57
14. Past and Future Are Present Ideas   60
15. Investigating the Mind   62
16. It Is Done   65
17. Things Are Free to Flow   67

| | | |
|---|---|---|
| 18. | One Substance | 70 |
| 19. | Clarity Does Not Come and Go | 72 |
| 20. | The Answer Is Not in the Mind | 74 |
| 21. | Mental Activity Versus Self-Centered Thinking | 76 |
| 22. | Focusing on Thoughts | 80 |
| 23. | Presence-Awareness Needs No Help | 83 |
| 24. | Knowing That You Are Cannot Be Doubted | 87 |
| 25. | Communicating with Others | 89 |
| 26. | Awareness Is the Constant Background of Experiences | 91 |
| 27. | The Separate 'I' Is the Root Concept | 93 |
| 28. | You Are Not an Appearance in the Mind | 95 |
| 29. | What Are We Looking For? | 98 |
| 30. | No 'Me' Left at All | 99 |
| 31. | The Mind Creates All Doubts and Problems | 100 |
| 32. | The Obviousness of 'What Is' | 101 |
| 33. | Self-Centered Stories | 104 |
| 34. | Emptiness and Nothingness | 105 |
| 35. | What You Are and What You Are Not | 107 |
| 36. | Recognizing Things in Awareness | 111 |
| 37. | Flip-Flopping | 112 |
| 38. | Pause Thought and Simply Be | 114 |
| 39. | There Is No Realization | 116 |
| 40. | Love, Joy, Peace and Happiness | 119 |
| 41. | Your Awareness Is Not in a Book | 121 |
| 42. | Life Flows Effortlessly | 123 |
| 43. | The Game Is Up | 124 |
| 44. | The End of the Story | 127 |
| 45. | Awareness and Seeing | 129 |
| 46. | Without You, the Universe Is Not | 131 |
| 47. | Are You Free of the False Sense of Self? | 132 |
| 48. | All Words Are Pointers | 136 |
| 49. | Becoming More Present? | 138 |
| 50. | The Separate Self Is Removed from the Equation | 140 |
| 51. | The Separate 'I' Is the Source of Suffering | 142 |
| 52. | Objects Appear, But You Exist | 145 |

| 53. | Ordinary, Present Awareness | 149 |
| 54. | You Are Awareness | 153 |
| 55. | Doer-ship Arises in the Question | 155 |
| 56. | Residual Doubts | 159 |
| 57. | I Am Already Here | 161 |
| 58. | There Is No Need to Fix Yourself | 165 |
| 59. | Do Not Turn this into a Project | 166 |
| 60. | Awareness Is Always 'On' | 168 |
| 61. | The 'Me' Is the First Illusion | 169 |
| 62. | Books Come and Go in Awareness | 171 |
| 63. | There Is No Expansion into Awareness | 173 |
| 64. | Start from the Position that You Are Already Free | 175 |
| 65. | Dealing with Practical Matters | 178 |
| 66. | Simply Being What You Are | 180 |
| 67. | No Awakening Is Needed | 181 |
| 68. | The Simplicity of Presence-Awareness | 185 |
| 69. | Doubts Are Thoughts in the Mind | 187 |
| 70. | What Good Does This Do Me? | 191 |
| 71. | Drop the Analysis of It | 194 |
| 72. | When the 'I' Is Not, There Are no More Troubles | 195 |
| 73. | The Suffering of Others | 196 |
| 74. | Something Clicked | 201 |
| 75. | Materialism, a Faith-Based Religion | 202 |
| 76. | Presence-Awareness and Perceptions | 206 |
| 77. | You Are the Answer | 208 |

Pointers 213
Addendum: *An Interview with John Wheeler* 229

# The Basics

# Review of the Basics

It all comes down to clarifying your identity. You are already present. So there is no need to look for a future state, experience or attainment. What you are seeking to know is not separate or distant, since it is your own self. What you are must be always with you. Anything which appears and disappears cannot, by definition, be what you are. Thoughts, feelings, perceptions, experiences, objects—these all come and go. None of them as such can be the essence of what you are. So set those aside and continue to look into your true nature. What is left to consider? Surprisingly little!

However, you are still present. You are still aware. Look at this presence of awareness itself. Having discarded all else, this is the only possible remainder and must be what you are. Your existence is beyond any doubt, and what you are is brightly aware. You are that knowing presence which is registering all thoughts, feelings and experiences. Look directly into this. This is the heart of the matter.

Notice that thoughts arise and set, but this presence—your own natural being—remains constant. There is no need to wait for the future to see this, nor is there any need for a special practice, technique or approach—simply because it is already present. You do not need to make an effort to be present and aware. It is completely natural and effortless. Look now and notice that what you are and the sense of presence-awareness are not two different things. You are that which is present and aware. Many words are used to point to this essential nature: presence, awareness, consciousness, life, spirit, emptiness, being, God, oneness and so on. These are all simply pointers. And what they are pointing to is your true nature—nothing more or less.

The body and mind may suffer experiences, yet awareness, your natural being, remains unaffected and uncompromised, just like the sun ever shining beyond the clouds and utterly untouched by them. Your true nature has no suffering, doubts or problems at all. See all this and you will find that your true nature is ever-present awareness, changeless being and undisturbed freedom and peace itself. These are additional pointers to the same wordless, immediate presence of your true nature.

You are not a limited, defective person, self or entity. This false belief is at the root of all seeking, suffering, doubts and problems in life. Those experiences are only creations of conceptual thought. Those concepts hinge on the imagined person who is assumed to be separate from oneness. So all thoughts of a suffering nature concern the identity, attributes and condition of a person to whom they are assumed to apply. Interest in the thoughts is sustained by the belief that we are that limited person, or separate self. The person to whom those thoughts and stories pertain is the central 'I thought', ego or person that we have assumed to be present and real. This is the 'lynch pin' of the whole production. All the self-centered concepts, beliefs and habits of mind are sustained by the belief in the presence of this person. That is why a very effective approach is simply to investigate the reality of this assumed person.

Where is the person? Is it real? Did you ever find it? For example, in any given moment there may be a few thoughts, feelings or sensations appearing. Do any of those constitute a person, a separate self? They are simply momentary objects appearing and disappearing in present awareness. How could they be a substantial self or independent person? If you set those aside and continue to investigate, you will find that there is nothing else present at all to investigate! All there is, is wide open, clear, obvious presence-awareness itself. And that is not a limited person or entity. The conclusion must be that the person that we have taken ourselves to be is a complete myth because it is not findable in direct experience. And if it does not exist now, then it never existed in the past, nor will it ever exist in the future.

If the person is discovered as not real, not present, a mere unexamined assumption, then the root of all self-centered, conceptual thoughts, beliefs, habits, and attachments is severed. With this recognition, the interest in the self-centered stories fades naturally and effortlessly because there is no more belief in the reality of the central concept, the person. The thoughts and beliefs unwind and scatter like autumn leaves in the wind. There is no more belief in the fixed reference point of a self or a central character. You simply remain as the open sky of awareness in which all thoughts arise and set—untouched, spacious, clear and always unmodified. The tendency to fixate on or attach to thoughts dissipates. Seeing this, you cannot believe in self-centered thoughts, even if you want to, because the basic misconception has been undermined. You do not seek water in a mirage once it is known to be a mirage.

What about the nature of the world, the universe that presents itself to us? All that we can know is what appears to us in immediate experience. And that which appears (whether it be a thought, feeling, perception or any other experience) has no separate and independent existence apart from the awareness which cognizes it. Since awareness and objects always appear together, they must be the same in essence. How many thoughts, feelings or perceptions can you have outside of awareness? They are inseparable. Everything that appears arises from, exists upon and returns into awareness. Even time, space and seeming external objects are present experiences contained in your knowing presence. There is nothing separate and apart from this—ever. In fact, there is just this—only this inescapable presence-awareness. You are that.

How do we live and function in the world? This is a false question because, as we have already seen, there is no one present who can live or function! At a practical level, all thoughts, feelings and actions go on without any reference to an imagined self-center or person. 'I' am not thinking, feeling, sensing, experiencing or acting because there is no 'I' present to do those things. Look at your thoughts right now. Is there an 'I' creating them? Or are they simply arising spontaneously? Surely the latter is the case. Do you have any idea what the next thought will be? If not, how can you say you created it? If you say you are choosing, creating or controlling your thoughts, then why would you ever create an unhappy or troubling thought? So you see that thoughts simply appear. There is no person or self involved at all. The same goes for choices, decisions, feelings and actions. It is all happening spontaneously. So the question 'How will I live my life?' is unnecessary. There is no 'you' to do anything at all. Things simply come up to be done. Life and its activities arise spontaneously and effortlessly from moment to moment in response to the demands of the situation and circumstances.

You can see all of these things directly. No special insight, awakening or enlightenment is needed. What is being pointed to is the natural condition of what is. We may have overlooked this, but it is not difficult to see. How could it be, when it is shining here in plain view? However, if necessary, you can review the basic points covered above and confirm them for yourself. Then the simple truth of your present natural state stands out very clearly right now. Before the next thought or experience appears you are already that natural and uncontrived presence-awareness itself.

# The Key Points

The purpose of non-dual spirituality is self-knowledge. When we look to see what we are, we find that the only thing that can qualify as our essential nature is the unchanging sense of our being, which is both existent and aware. In looking at this sense of being-awareness, we see that it is already here and easily recognized. Not only is it present, but it remains present and undisturbed in the midst of all thinking, feeling and experiencing. It is not something that comes to us as a future experience. It is not something that we get from a book or obtain as a result of practices, techniques or processes. Nor is it something that comes to us from outside, from a teacher, a divine being or any other source. We do not need an awakening or enlightenment experience to know our true nature. It is effortlessly present. In fact, there is nothing we can do to escape it. We have seen that our true nature is nothing objective, yet it is clearly evident beyond any doubt. We are not something apart from being-awareness—we ARE being-awareness. Thus, there is no separation between us and reality.

Finally, we have seen that this true nature, this essential awareness, is utterly and completely free of suffering, doubt, fear, worry and strife. Not only is it present and aware, but it is pure peace and freedom itself. For this reason, self-knowledge is not a matter of a deepening experience or of a stabilization in our true nature. That would only be in reference to an imagined difference between what we are and what we imagine we may become in the future. It also assumes the reality of time, as well as a separate being that would attain some special state of awakening or enlightenment. We have seen that these notions are dualistic. Self-knowledge is nothing if it is not a clear understanding of what already is. There is nothing beyond self-knowledge because self-knowledge is non-duality. All that appears is only an expression or appearance of the one, undivided, ever-present being-awareness. There is nothing beyond oneness. Nothing more is needed beyond self-knowledge because our true nature is this unalterable being, awareness and freedom that can never be contradicted under any circumstances.

# Questions for Self-Knowledge

**The Aim of Non-Duality—Self-Knowledge**

The central message of non-dual traditions comes down to the following proposition. The discovery of what is real and the resolution of suffering, seeking and doubt is obtained by a clear understanding of one's real nature. In short, the aim of spiritual endeavor is "self-knowledge."

By definition, whatever we are is already here. Therefore, the self to be known by self-knowledge must be already present in our immediate experience. Our being is not something distant or separate from who we are. It is who we are. In self-knowledge, we are not obtaining something new, but clarifying what is already present though perhaps not clearly known or fully appreciated. We are not waiting for a future experience in which we will obtain something that we do not yet have. Nor are we waiting to achieve a special state of "enlightenment," "awakening" or anything else of the sort. The point is simply to clarify one's already-present nature.

**What We Are Not—and What We Are**

The first step is to get a basic sense of what our identity could be. Whatever we are must be constantly with us. The qualities of our essential nature must be invariably present in who we are. Things which arise and pass away or undergo change cannot be essential characteristics of ourselves. Given this premise, none of the following can be the essence of what we are because they all appear and disappear:

- Thoughts
- Feelings
- Sensations
- Perceptions
- Experiences
- States
- Perceived objects

These are all appearances that come and go. None of them stays constant in our direct experience. For this reason, they do not qualify as "candidates" for our real nature. So we must set them aside as not being the essence of what we are. What remains? Is there anything else left? One might conclude that there is nothing else left to consider. If this is true, our real nature must be non-existent. But this conclusion is premature. There is still something more to consider. First, there is a sense of being, the sense that "we are." In spite of the ever-changing flow of experiences, we also know that we are present, that we exist. We know that we remain present in and through the changing experiences. Otherwise, how could we know the presence of changing experiences? Furthermore, this presence is not void or inert. It is conscious, cognizant, aware. This sense of being present and aware must be what we are because it is the only possible remainder after all the other possibilities have been exhausted.

This investigation provides the essential clue about what is to be known in self-knowledge. It is our present true identity, the essential characteristic of which is to be present and aware. We are and we are aware. As will become clear in what follows, we are not dealing with two different things here (that is, presence and awareness). Instead we are acknowledging one principle that can be viewed in different ways or pointed to with different labels, all of which refer to the same basic essence.

To clarify terms, when referring to the sense of being present, the following terms are used interchangeably: "presence," "being," "existence" or "the sense that you are." When referring to the awareness aspect of our nature, the following terms are used: "awareness," "consciousness," "cognizance" or "knowing," among others. In addition, because we are dealing with a single principle or phenomenon (our true nature), hyphenated terms are sometimes used, such as "presence-awareness," "being-awareness," "being-consciousness," "aware-presence" and so on. In all cases, the pointers refer to the same principle, your essential true nature.

So our true nature is that principle within us that is present and aware. Once we have this insight, we are in a position to have a good look and fully appreciate what this present true nature is.

## The Questions—A Means to Approach Direct, Non-Conceptual Recognition

The following series of questions are provided to highlight various facets of your real being. They will serve to flesh out the recognition of what you already are, which is fully present but perhaps not fully appreciated. When considering the questions, look in your immediate experience and respond from your own direct, non-conceptual, non-theoretical knowing. By answering these questions for yourself, various aspects of your true nature will come clearly into view, not based on theory or speculation, but through direct, first-hand knowing.

[1] Can you recognize the sense that you are present, that you are? And, further, can you recognize the fact of awareness?

Comment: The facts of being present and being aware are intuitively and directly obvious, even without any reflection.

No one can say "I am not." Even to assert that you are not, you must be present to make the assertion. As for awareness, clearly all thoughts, feelings, sensations and experiences are being known. They are registering in some principle of knowing or cognition. Otherwise, how could we know of them or speak of them? No one can say that awareness is not present because the very assertion arises as an object in present awareness.

[2] Did you need to think to note the fact of being and awareness?

Comment: Notice that when you are questioned about the sense of being or the capacity of awareness, you can immediately and intuitively affirm the presence of both of these. You do not need to reference thought or engage the use of reason in order to respond. Even before the mind activates in order to express an answer, the positive answer is already known. This shows that the recognition of the true nature of the self is not a product of thinking. It is immediate, non-conceptual knowing. If you are in the habit of using the mind as your primary instrument or tool of knowing, this point may not be obvious. This is because the mind deals in concepts. Being is not a concept. Awareness is not a concept. In truth, the mind has no capacity to recognize your true nature. This is why one often hears statements such as "the answer is not in the mind" and "the mind cannot understand this" and so forth.

[3] Notice the fact of being present and aware. Also notice that various thoughts, feelings, sensations and experiences are arising and setting in this aware presence. As you notice these changing experiences, does the sense of being present and aware change at all? Does it disappear? Does it waver? Does it come and go?

Comment: Not only is the sense of being-awareness present now, but the presence or absence of thoughts, feelings, sensations and other experiences does not affect this in any way. Your presence remains unmodified and undisturbed in and through all appearances. Begin to notice this for yourself. We are generally so captivated by experiences that we completely overlook the being-awareness that is the necessary background for them all. For example, how many thoughts, feelings or perceptions can you have without the presence of your existence and awareness?

[4] Do you have to wait for the future to recognize this (meaning, the sense of being and awareness)?

Comment: You do not wait for the future to know the fact of being and the presence of awareness. Being and awareness do not happen in the future. They are present facts. Your true nature is not something that will arrive as a future event or experience. Being-awareness, which we have already determined to be our essential nature, is already here.

An important implication of this is that any spiritual approach that relies on time or posits some attainment in the future is evidently dualistic and out of harmony with the basic message of non-duality. The aim of non-dual teachings is clear self-recognition. Our true nature or essential self does not reside in the future. Therefore, any doctrine which relies on a future state or condition, even if that be termed an awakening or enlightenment event, is operating in the realm of duality.

[5] Do you need to take up a practice, technique or exercise to recognize being-awareness?

Comment: In order to recognize present being-awareness is any technique, process or exercise necessary? The answer must be negative. You do not need to do anything to be present. You do not have to do anything to generate awareness. In fact, it is quite the reverse—in order to do or undertake anything, the sense of existence-awareness must be already present as a prerequisite. Those who are practicing, striving and exerting themselves in order to attain some spiritual goal have the cart before the horse. Self-knowledge, which is the recognition of your true nature, is not the result of a practice. Practices may be useful for relative achievements and accomplishments, but they are entirely useless in the case of self-knowledge. In fact, they are worse than useless, because by pursuing such practices we are actively denying the essential recognition that our true nature is here and now.

[6] Do you need to read a spiritual book to recognize being-awareness?

Comment: Is it necessary to read a book to notice the fact of being and its natural capacity of awareness? You must answer in the negative. Many of us have searched in spiritual books in hopes of discovering the truth of who we are. But your self is not in a book, so no amount of looking there will bring you closer to knowing who you are. The only real value books (or any other pointers) can have is to point out the need for knowing that principle of being-awareness that is present within us. No objective looking or searching is needed for the clear and simple knowing of our true nature.

[7] Does someone come and give this (being-awareness) to you or is it already here?

Comment: Many of us are under the impression that the recognition of who we are comes from the influence of something or someone outside of ourselves. This could be through a teacher, through the grace of a god or some other intervention. But is it true that someone or something descends upon us and delivers being-awareness to us? The fact of being-awareness is already available. Nothing needs to be brought in from the outside.

[8] Do you need to have a special "awakening" or "enlightenment" experience to see this, your present being and awareness?

Comment: As seekers, many of us assumed that self-knowledge implies some special spiritual insight or attainment, some extraordinary state of consciousness or moment of understanding. But do you have to have any awakening or enlightenment experience to know the fact of being-awareness? While waiting for some hoped-for enlightenment or awakening, we are missing the fact that what is being pointed to is already completely present.

[9] Do you need to make an effort to be present and aware?

Comment: Are you making any effort at all to be or to be aware? You do not struggle to be present and aware. They are not something that you do. These are naturally present and involve no effort at all.

[10] Can you do anything to stop being present and aware?

Comment: Not only are being and awareness effortlessly and naturally present, but there is nothing you can do to stop them, eradicate them or cancel them. You cannot turn them off, even if you want to. No amount of activity on your part can make being-awareness disappear. So not only is our true nature of being-awareness already present, but there is nothing we can do to lose it.

[11] Is your sense of being, this aware presence, something you can grasp hold of as an object?

Comment: Is your sense of being-awareness something that you perceive "out there" as something objective, apart from yourself? Is that essential awareness a thought, feeling or experience that you can point to and say "there it is"? You cannot point to being or awareness as "things," as objects standing before you. Being-awareness has no particular form, shape or dimension. Being-awareness is not an object. It cannot be grasped by the mind (as a thought) or by the senses (as a perceived object), and yet it is most clearly present. Its presence is utterly beyond doubt.

We tend to overlook the truth of who we are because our being cannot be known through the instruments of knowledge we are accustomed to using. If you attempt to understand your true nature through the senses or mind, you will miss it. However, once you grasp this basic point, you can let go using the senses and mind to understand your true nature and rely upon non-conceptual, immediate knowing.

You are and you know that you are. This itself is recognizing your true nature. This is not simply knowing, as if you were knowing some objective fact, but it is also being. You are what you know and you know what you are. This is a unique phenomenon in which what is knowing and what is being known are one and the same thing. Being is, and being knows itself. For this reason, our essential nature is sometimes referred to as "self-knowing awareness."

[12] In your direct experience, is it that you are one thing and existence-awareness is something else "over there" and apart? Or is it that you ARE that which is present and aware?

Comment: The point here is that being-awareness is not a principle separate from us. It is not that we are here and being-awareness is somewhere "over there." Rather, we are that which is present and aware. Being-awareness is non-separate from who we are. It is what we are. This means that what we are and the principle of being-awareness are not two different things. This shows that the "goal" of the non-dual teachings is not a distant objective. The real aim is the revelation of what we are. Our true nature and the ultimately real essence of things are one and the same. This is non-duality. This is why there is no path, no goal and no attainment—because what we have been seeking is what we already are.

Our true nature is ever present, beyond the need for seeking and impossible to lose. It is already the case. The only issue was that we did not appreciate what was already here. And this is why there is no possibility of deepening, stabilizing, growing into it and so forth. All such notions are clearly rooted in the subtle concept of separation or duality. Only an imagined entity that is separate and apart from the reality can dream of deepening, stabilizing or what have you. In the clear seeing of the facts, all of those notions are discarded as conceptual errors based on ignorance. Identity does not become more identical. Awareness does not become more aware. Existence does not become more existent. You do not become more of what you already are.

[13] It is granted that bodies and minds suffer various experiences, such as pleasure and pain, activity and calm and so on. But does existence-awareness (your true nature) as such suffer any of these experiences in its intrinsic nature?

Comment: Notice that the body, mind and senses all have experiences. These experiences unfold in the realm of appearances and are dualistic in nature. For example, the body may experience pleasure or pain. But does awareness, your real essence, experience pleasure or pain? No, because it is the body that has those experiences. Awareness, in itself, is quite free and untouched. It is not subject to either pleasure or pain. Consider the mind. The mind may experience doubt or certainty, fear or safety, troubles or contentment. These are clearly mental states. But does awareness suffer any of these experiences? In other words, is it touched or affected by these mental states? Again you will see that it is the mind that is affected, but not your true nature of awareness.

What does this mean? It means that your true nature is totally free of suffering, pain, doubt, fear, problems, questions, concerns and so forth. It is also free of the opposites of all these things. What you are is beyond all pain, suffering and doubt. But this is only describing your true nature in terms of what it is not. On the positive side, we can say that it is undisturbed peace, fullness and wholeness that can never be lost or compromised. Why? Because this is the intrinsic nature of our real self. This point illuminates another key facet of our true nature. Not only is our essential being present and aware, but it is also unconditional peace, happiness, and freedom.

Our only "problem," if one may say so, was not appreciating this that we truly are and ever have been. None of this arrives as a future attainment. It is realized to be the ongoing and ever-present condition of what is. We are only acknowledging the nature of what we already are. That is why there does not need to be a deepening or stabilizing, but only a recognition of something that already is. All approaches that rely on gradual attainment, deepening, stabilizing and so on are still in terms of the illusion that we are something that we are not. The only emphatic remedy is clear self-knowledge. There is no attainment beyond self-knowledge because the self, our essential being, is perfect wholeness and absolute freedom. Who you are is non-separate from the one reality itself. There is nothing beyond non-duality.

[14] Does any appearance (thought, feeling, sensation, object,

state or experience) exist independent or separate from presence-awareness?

Comment: Everything that we ever know or experience appears within presence-awareness. You have never had a single thought, feeling, sensation or any other experience outside of awareness. In other words this presence-awareness is the necessary precondition for anything else to be. Without this conscious presence nothing else is. Because objects of experience and the presence of awareness are never known independently of each other, they must be, in essence, the same undivided substance or principle. Just as waves are nothing but water or gold ornaments are nothing but gold, so are all appearances nothing but that one undeniable being-awareness. All that appears, including the seeker himself, is only that.

# Why Did Separation Ever Arise?

If you look at negative thoughts, they revolve around a notion that we are separate, limited and incomplete. They all hang on this root belief. So the common sense approach is to look at that core belief and see if it is true and confirm what our true nature actually is. That is the practical resolution of the issue. Then there are no more questions and doubts. To resolve this matter through clear understanding is the best use of one's energy and curiosity. All else is a delaying tactic. No matter how much you try to get to first causes, you must still clarify this basic misunderstanding in the end.

As to why the ignorant notion of separation ever arose in the first place, a practical answer might be that from a young age we were conditioned by a wrong belief, which we innocently took as true. Everything else evolved from this. There is no real explanation for why the notion of separation arose because any bit of looking shows that such a condition is not the case. There is no separation at all. Seeing this, the root is addressed and all delusive notions are undercut here and now. Ignorance and suffering have a cause, but when you investigate the cause, you find that the cause is not present. It is a false assumption. The separation from source never happened. So there can be no explanation for why separation occurred, because it never did. It is a false question. You do not answer a false question. You see it as false and discard it.

From another angle you can say that with the rise of the potential for conceptual, abstract thinking, the mind developed the capacity to formulate notions like 'I' and 'mine'. The mind took its own creations for substantial, real entities. Then it got a bit lost in it own concepts—for a time. But awareness has not been entangled or bound by these errors of the mind. In fact, it is what is seeing this and motivating the return to the clear vision of things.

One final angle on this. 'Why?' implies causality. It means 'What is the reason?' 'How did this occur?' 'When did this occur?' 'What was the motivation?' These are clearly thoughts in the mind. The belief in causality is driving these questions. That is to say, causality is taken as valid. But causality itself is a creation of thought. It applies to the world of appearances. Outside of the mind, you cannot speak of causality as such because it only applies after the mind is present and has created notions of time, space and agency. So to asking 'why did the thought of separation ever arise?' assume that before the mind was present causality was in operation. So it is a false question.

At a young age the notion of separation was thrust on the mind and taken as true. But this can be re-examined and resolved now. Then there are no longer any problems. In seeing this, the questions, doubts and suffering fall away. You are perfect and completely free right now because there is no actual separation from source.

# Memory

Memory comes up in the form of thoughts and images in the present moment like any other thought activity. So memory is a form of thought. Memories are present thoughts that arise and pass in present-moment awareness. Practically speaking, memory seems to be a function that ties together, coordinates and recalls former thoughts. It appears to store concepts and images and bring them forth. Conditioned beliefs, such as the notion of being a separate self and all the related identifications, survive in memory. Without memory, they have no substance, no continuity, no real existence. So, in a sense, you can say that all our problems are due to the capacity of memory. All of our beliefs, points of view and assumptions appear to be stored there. Furthermore, the reference point of a fixed 'I', thinker or self only resides in memory.

Memory as a thing in itself is hard to pin down. It is like the concept of 'the mind'. Where is 'the mind'? There are thoughts passing through awareness, but where is 'the mind' apart from that? It is the same with memory. We posit such a function or entity, but where is it apart from the presently arising thoughts? It just so happens that we label some presently occurring thoughts as memories. Then we assume a past to which those memories refer. In this way, a whole conceptual world is spun up in thoughts. But they are all occurring here and now in present awareness. It is castles in air being constructed in thought. In a moment, we are conceiving of a past time, a past world, a past entity that was in that world, a memory to hold all that and ourselves as some of kind being present in the middle of all of it. But take a deeper look and see what is going on. In present awareness, present thoughts are appearing and disappearing. It is all purely conceptual, purely imagined. Time, the external world and the separate entity are all posited in thought. They are taken as real, but are not actually present as substantial things in themselves.

This is easy to see in the case of a dream. You fall into a dream state. In that dream state, you have a discussion with a friend about something you did together five years ago (in the dream). A normal conversation occurs and you and your dream friend discuss various events that happened. Appropriate memories appear to corroborate everything. When you wake up you look back and see that it was all fabricated in the mind in the moment of dreaming. There was no past at all. Not to mention that there were no real dream characters either! It was all appearances taken as real. However, awareness stands beyond, free and untouched. It is not even in the dream. The dream is in it. It suffers no limitations occurring in the dream. The awareness itself is no limited appearance in the dream. It is not any particular entity or object in the dream. It is the same with our present awareness in this apparent waking state.

Conventionally, you can say that the mind creates the notion of a substantial, independent self and that this belief is sustained in memory. There is no harm in that as far as it goes. But the truth is that it is all simply present thoughts. And there is no separate thinker or 'me' to be found. Your actual identity is that space-like, utterly free awareness itself. All self-centered thoughts are baseless, as there is no one to whom they apply. See this clearly and there is really nothing else needed. It is the heart of the matter. Seeing this, suffering, doubt, seeking and personal problems vanish entirely.

## Ongoing Practice?

Seeing your fundamental identity and the absence of the conceptual entity or person who is separate undercuts the need for an ongoing process or a maintenance approach to things. The body-mind is simply an appearance, a flow of energy, if you will. The notions that appearances are 'powerful', 'difficult', 'turbulent', 'dreadful' and need to be managed or integrated are conceptual interpretations. This stems from putting an unnecessary amount of focus on them. See them for what they are—ephemeral, insubstantial appearances. Emotions and feelings are waves of energy, spontaneous appearances in awareness. They only seem significant when focused on. Otherwise, they are seen as they truly are, just passing states arising in clear, problem-free awareness. They are neither right nor wrong. There is nothing to fix or correct because, ultimately, there is nothing substantial present.

The past is non-existent. The future is non-existent. That only leaves whatever handful of thoughts and feelings are arising presently. They come and go in an instant because they have no real substance. So what is to fix, integrate or heal? This is especially the case when you see that those things are not your identity. There is no self, no entity present. So not only is there no real objective problem, but there is no person present to have a problem. This way of looking resolves any lingering anxiety about appearances.

Once you see that you, as a limited person, do not exist and that, therefore, no appearances can be related to a self-center, then the tendency to focus on thoughts and emotions dissipates. Much less are you inclined to put energy into labeling them. Emotional energies in themselves are impersonal. They do not carry inherent value judgments, such as 'good' or 'painful'. Those are all conceptual overlays put on by the mind.

Simply let things remain unmodified, unaltered and uncorrected. With a clear view of your real nature and the undermining of the belief in the false self, you find there is not much interest in relating emotional states to the saga of a person who needs to be fixed. Then the emotional energies come to their own natural balance. The clarification of the fundamentals tackles this type of issue at the roots, rather than dealing with effects. Beliefs, problems, blockages and so on are effects of unexamined views and assumptions. When these are addressed, the effects usually resolve naturally.

There is no ongoing practice because there is no time and no person. You are not separate from oneness or totality. So what practice is needed and who is to do it? Who says that emotions are right or wrong, pleasant or painful? Who decided that things need to be integrated or that there is more work to do? From the position of oneness all is a spontaneous appearance. If something comes up to be done or corrected in the body and mind, that will come up. There need not be any anxiety about it.

# Take the Focus Off of the Mind

All that can ever happen is that some thoughts and feelings arise momentarily and disappear. They are ephemeral dream stuff, really. They appear in the clear, solid and unwavering light of your being. Your being is not a thought. It is not contained by thought. So, acknowledge this presence and let your consideration return to it. It is already free, open and clear—just like the sky is free of the passing clouds.

Thoughts and feelings never causes suffering. How can they, since they do not really touch you? They are gone in a moment. Our only trouble is being fascinated with them because we take them as true. Suffering thoughts are self-centered stories in the mind about a poor, defective 'me' that is separate, apart, incomplete. We suffer because we focus on these thoughts. Otherwise, they pass through without a hitch. The thoughts survive because they refer to a separate self we take to be present and real. Stop right now and look in your experience. Is there any actual defective person here? Do you see one? Or are there only a few thoughts and feelings passing through? There is nothing else here. The defective person that is driving our fixation on thought is a myth. All that is here is spacious, open and luminous awareness itself. Seeing this burns off all mental and emotion fog.

Take the focus off of the mind. Take a walk. Look at the sky, the trees, the land. Notice how awareness encompasses it all. Conceptual thought is just a small part of everything going on. Be alive to the whole field of awareness. This reduces the fixation on ephemeral thoughts. Do whatever works for you to snap out of keeping focused on thoughts and feelings. They will pass. You will remain.

*Dialogues with John*

# 1
## Who Is Aware of Thought?

*Question: The natural state is pure awareness, not my awareness but just beingness. So far, so good. But that awareness does not register in deep sleep nor presumably in death. So what is eternal about it? And how can one know it when dead or anesthetized? Several events happened in my life when there was no 'me'. There was just being, seeing and hearing with no sense of 'me', but the body and mind were definitely awake. In deep sleep or under anesthetic, there is no awareness, presence, being or consciousness. So is presence, the natural state, only registering when the body-mind is awake and alive?*

John: It is not true that you cease to exist or be aware in sleep. The mind and senses are in abeyance. That is all. If a thought, dream or sensation appears in deep sleep, you, as presence-awareness, are there to register it. It is easy to see this here and now in the waking state. Thoughts and experiences are arising and setting constantly. Do you cease to be present and aware as the thoughts appear and disappear? Who observes the passing of a thought? When the thought is gone, do you cease to be present and aware? Not at all!

We overlook the simple fact of the unchanging presence of our real nature due to being identified with and focused on objects. But your real nature is not an object. Can you really say that you come and go as the thoughts come and go? Where are you in the moment between two thoughts? Can you say you are not? Sleep is just an extended moment, so to speak, between thoughts or experiences. If you have not disappeared between two thoughts, neither have you disappeared in sleep. All talk of sleep is theoretical, as we are talking about a hypothetical state, from the point of view of the present moment. You, as presence-awareness, are here and now. You can see what you are now rather than worry about other states and conditions.

Keep it simple. You are present and aware. This is beyond doubt. Feel your way into this doubtless presence that you are. All other considerations take you into conceptual thought and away from what is being pointed to.

# 2
## There Is No One Apart from This

*Question: I am still in bit of a quandary over this so-called 'ordinariness'. I am wondering about the 'juice'. I know that in all this wondering there is still a 'me' that is looking to be seen, trying to fool me once again. I know that any feeling of lack, including wanting more juicy stuff, has to be based on the assumed sense of 'I'. When the 'me' appears in the form of wanting something it feels it does not have, do you continue with the inquiry? It feels like this is the case. I mean, thoughts keep rising.*

John: Is there anything wrong with the awareness shining right here and now? Thoughts, feelings and experiences come and go, but can you deny the space of knowing presence that is illuminating it all? And are you separate from that? The existence that you are is life, light, presence, love—unfathomably deep and rich. It is the source from which all arises and into which it all sets. Can there be a mind, a body or a world apart from presence-awareness? It is the heart of being, the source of knowing, the source from which everything springs. It is the substance from which all is made. You are that essence. There is no one and no thing apart from this. Some call it God, spirit, source or love. It is the very essence of existence and life.

Simply recognize this undeniable and inescapable presence of awareness that you are. All life, peace, clarity and joy are in that. These are all aspects of the true nature that you are. Settle in with the recognition that your own true nature is not other than this presence-awareness. It appears subtle to the mind used to gross sensations and experiences. Be willing to stay with that subtleness. You will find immense depth in it. All else is simply thoughts and objects appearing in this awareness that you are. The sense of knowing presence is what you are and remain as, no matter how many thoughts and ideas arise.

The notion of being something apart from presence-awareness is the root concept that sustains the belief in a sense of separate selfhood. However, there is no 'me', and no separate self at all. All the notions, beliefs and desires that are built on this false idea are also false. When attention wanders onto these ideas and beliefs, the imagined identity is given reality and your identity as doubtless presence-awareness is overlooked. However, when this is looked into, you immediately see that the whole thing is a conceptual house of cards. It falls to pieces with a only bit of examination.

There is no 'me' or 'I' to be gotten rid of. It is pointed out as an assumption that has no existence. If there is no 'I', then who needs to do anything? All the problems are for the seeming separate self. So, you tell me, just where is this thing?

Thoughts arise. Of course! The wind blows, clouds appear, activities happen, objects show up on the screen of awareness. There is no problem. It is all swirling around in presence-awareness, which is your real nature. Those experiences do not affect your true nature at all.

All trouble comes from losing sight of what we are. Be what you are and what is the trouble? Why give any weight to the old concepts that there is a problem, that you are not there yet, that there is a practice needed to be what you are? It is tempting to believe that a carrot is dangling at the end of the stick. We have spent enough time going around that track! Have a look at the whole mechanism and simply see the true facts. Look for yourself and tell me, from your direct experience, what is the nature of this presence-awareness that you are? Somehow, I do not think you will say that it is bland, ordinary or lacks 'juice'. All the great spiritual traditions are only describing your true nature—vast, empty, free, peaceful, unchanging, one with all, the source, light, life, love, beauty, truth. Remember the immense treasure that lies within, that nameless essence that is undeniably present and aware in you.

Old thoughts and concepts may arise due to habit and years of pampering them. Simply see them as baseless ideas shining right in the true essence that you are. That essence is completely present, whole and complete right now. This is your birthright, your home, your native ground. Refuse to grant belief to concepts, and take your stand on what is undeniable and present in you. Look at everything from this perspective. This puts everything into proper focus. The apparent separate entity is a total fiction. It has never existed, except as an assumption. That which does not exist and has never been present does not need to be fixed, corrected or made complete. Nor can such an imagined thing knock you out of your true nature. A bit of looking shows that presence-awareness is what is real and that you have never, ever been apart from this. Seeing this, it is clear that all problems are imaginary. They are baseless assumptions taken as true. They are completely annihilated with simple looking and questioning.

You are and you know you are. If there is any doubt, then come back and see for yourself what is true about who you are. Take your stand there.

# 3
## Follow the Insights Back to Your Real Nature

*Question: I had an insight about thoughts of the past and future. I realized forcefully and for the first time that right now is the only reality there is to inquire about. The rest is just thoughts. Therefore, my present consciousness is that reality. I need not worry about anything else. That freed me up to be conscious of the availability of my awareness at any time. I do not want to try to label it too much. I have seen too many people make grand and mystifying announcements about their sudden states of grace, which turn out to be only passing experiences. I now see awareness itself. I see its qualities of depth, space, beauty and peace beginning to show.*

*At the same time, I still worry about my problems and wish I did not have to do anything that involves conflict or actual work! I really want to grasp what the pointers are about, and I believe that 'effortless living' is really possible with this understanding. I do not mean having no challenges, but resolving problems more easily and confidently. It seems key to not expect emotions, conflicts and problems to dissolve or go away. Even when abiding in love, people are just people. They slip up and do things that are not so nice. And some people only think they understand, but are off on another ego trip. It is up to each of us to decide how to relate to purported teachers or students claiming understanding. Most of all, it is up to us to realize that life goes on, even with the understanding. It is not a ticket to fly to the moon and play among the stars!*

John: Follow the insights back to your actual nature, which is doubtlessly present and aware. Through all the seeming ups and downs and ins and outs, you have never lost your true nature, nor has the innate and natural awareness that you are ceased to shine. You are present and aware. That is fully clear, fully here now. From the point of view of the mind, it is a seeming no thing. Awareness? So what, we may say! From the point of view of direct recognition or knowing, it is open, clear, free and untouched by whatever appears. As I say, it is not that 'we' get free. Rather, it is that we discover that we are inherently and always free. We were only looking into the mind and taking ourselves to be what we were not. Focusing on the stories and thoughts in the mind, we overlooked what was clear and present and shining right here in plain view. To reclaim our identity as that presence-awareness is the essence of it all.

Yes, thoughts and activities go on. Why not? Where is the problem in any of it? None of it is a problem. None of it binds until we begin to interpret it through the filters of thought and belief based on the limited sense of self. Even so, it is only mind stuff. Nothing is really happening at all! Those thoughts rise and set right in the presence that you are. When recognition remains with our true nature, all the fixation on self-centered concepts drops away. We remain in and as that simple sense of presence. It is quite simple, so simple we are apt to discount it. But at some point, the evidence of our own direct experience is overwhelming.

Life, thoughts and day-to-day activities spontaneously appear, swirl around and float through. There is absolutely no problem with any of it. There is no need to posit a sense of personal self in the picture. There is no need to assume a problematic 'you' with an issue. The seeming person that we take ourselves to be is not really present. Of course there are thoughts, actions, preferences and activities, but there is no one present to whom they are happening, only the open space of awareness itself.

Who you have imagined yourself to be is a make-believe character, a fictional creation in the mind. Where is she if you are not thinking about her? Our misunderstanding is taking that fabrication to be who we are. The whole essence of this is to see that false assumption as false, and to see the truth of what we are. You are not and never were a fictional character created in the mind. You are and always have been that bright, clear, open space of presence-awareness in which everything appears and disappears. It is so simple that we overlook it. For a time, we continue to favor the beliefs in the mind about ourselves over the direct recognition of our real nature as it is. Then we see that we cannot possibly be a concept. No thought or experience is what we are. We cease to believe in the mental picture of ourselves and relax into the pure knowingness that we truly are. This is the natural state. We are in that state now. We simply see the truth of this.

Worries and doubts are only thoughts appearing in the mind. They have no real substance and do not really touch us. Settle in with the knowing of what you are and the interest and belief in the mind-created thoughts withers away. Such thoughts are not a problem. You deal with whatever comes up in a practical and straightforward way, to the best of your ability. There is less and less inclination to interpret events and experiences through the point of view of a problematic, separate self. Why keep up all that hard work when you can simply relax and effortlessly remain as that presence-awareness that you cannot leave?

# 4
## This Is Easy and Effortless

*Question: I recently discovered your website and decided to listen to your interview with Allin Taylor. Your simple description of your meeting with 'Sailor' Bob Adamson shifted my perspective radically. I suddenly saw the simple truth in it all. I realized the natural state that I had been seeking was awareness itself.*

John: This is key.

*Q: I had been thinking that awareness was what led to the natural state rather than seeing that it was the natural state itself. Over the next few days being aware was relatively easy.*

John: It is one hundred percent easy and effortless. It is going on all the time. It is not a state you achieve. It is the natural state. Natural means effortless. It is not a maintenance state.

*Q: My life just seemed to flow, with actions being taken as and when required, seemingly without any input from me. It also seemed like there was nothing else that needed answering.*

John: This is the natural condition, the normal state. You experienced this directly. The direct recognition of who and what you are undercuts the false concepts based on the belief in being a separate, limited person or entity. What you saw and experienced was the gist of it. Do not overlook the importance of this.

*Q: One of the things that occurred to me was the feeling that everything was okay at the moment. But what happens when events in my life take a downward turn? I try to treat this lightly and look upon it as another thought, consoling myself with the fact that when that happens it is just another experience and that I should not give it any more significance than anything else in my life.*

John: You need a clear understanding of what is going on if you are going to be truly free of it. You may try to dismiss the thoughts, but if you have not clearly seen the underlying causes generating them, they will return.

Q: A reoccurring background problem that I do seem to have is my dislike for my current employment. I am a computer programmer, but after over twenty years in the industry, I find that I have little motivation for doing it anymore, other than I am relatively well paid for what I do. I am experiencing a crisis, in as much as I am almost at the point of being fired for lack of performance! I cannot seem to act one way or another, which is causing me to suffer, as you may imagine. The real problem seems to be the fact that I cannot rationalize my apparent dilemma with being in the natural state. I seem to see events taking place and have no interest in them whatsoever. That very fact itself is causing me anguish. It is almost like I am watching a film of a train wreck happening. Can you offer some light on the situation?

John: Be very clear that the problem is not in the objective events. Your body will work or not, determined by the circumstances. There is absolutely no problem with it. If a change needs to happen it will. All the doubts and suffering are generated in thought, based on how the mind is framing things. See that all suffering is created in the mind. You have a sense of what it means to be the natural state of awareness. But how, where and why the suffering arises is yet to be fully understood. It is not difficult, but requires some looking and inquiry to see the mechanism of it. When this is understood, the outer events will sort themselves out effortlessly and will not be a problem. There is definitely an answer and resolve to your dilemma. How do I know? I went through a similar situation myself. Looking at these pointers cleared things up completely. It can work for you, too.

[Follow up]

*Q: Thank you for your extensive response. In the short time since my original email, I managed to work through several of the issues by realizing that, as you confirmed, awareness is key. I realized that the problems I mentioned were part of my conditioned response system to my experiences. I could see that my mind felt no need to act when I had good or neutral experiences but did not like it when my experience was evaluated as bad. My mind then went into a strategy of actions to try to get itself back to a place that it perceived as comfortable. By being aware and observing my experiences, I could see that no experience was better or worse than any other. Your comments seemed to confirm this.*

*I am beginning to see that, as you say, awareness is key. All other issues of understanding are beginning to fall into place. I feel like there is a consolidation process going on with a 'mopping up' of secondary issues being resolved as and when they arise. I only need to remain with my natural state and not let the mind divert me. Thank you once more for your help.*

# 5

## Do Whatever Comes Up Next

*Question: I had a wonderful time in Australia. As for my talks with Bob Adamson, I do not have a lot to say aside from—you were right. I talked with Bob for about an hour a day when I was there. My doubts and questions were systematically undermined until things became quite clear. My dialogues with you last year were a good preparation, probably making Bob's job a lot easier!*

*The mind is now jabbering away with questions such as 'What to do now?' 'Should I make some attempt to try to share this?' 'Should I try to articulate thoughts around this?' 'Can the search really be over?' 'What search?' and so on. But the thoughts are easily seen through as having no real reference point. The feeling of concern that usually accompanied such thoughts previously seems no longer to be there. It is hard to articulate. Any articulation of 'it' must necessarily fail miserably. Does a way of expressing this naturally arise as the understanding sets in? I do not feel a strong motivation to 'hang out a shingle' and start talking about this. At the same time, I am willing to share the understanding with anyone who might find it helpful.*

*Thanks again for everything, John. I feel a tremendous gratitude to you and Bob Adamson. You were like brothers who welcomed me home after a long and difficult trip.*

John: I am glad to hear all is well and settling in. Basically, there is no need to worry about anything. I had the same questions for Bob Adamson after seeing him, to which he pointedly replied, 'Just do whatever comes up next!' It was a simple but comprehensive point. There is no issue because thoughts and experiences come up spontaneously with no reference to a self-center. Who is choosing anything? Where is the problem with any of it? Stay with the basic recognition of what you are, and from there everything takes care of itself. If you are going to share this, you will. If not now, then you will not. Follow your heart and intuition. The intelligence within you will bring up whatever is bound to come up to do. From the ultimate view, it does not matter, because you are what you are, regardless. Enjoy the presentation of whatever arises in the field of awareness. You will marvel how all things naturally unfold, and you will see the underlying harmony and inevitability of whatever happens.

*Q: Thank you for the thoughts. There is a bit of wavering, but for the most part there is hardly any concern about things like there used to be. I will definitely keep in touch.*

John: All sounds fine. You are what you are and you know what you are. The only thing that can potentially come up are some residual habits of mind from the past based on the belief in being what we are not. They come up from time to time and are seen. It is only thoughts. What you are is never touched in the slightest. Once you have gotten a feel for all this, you cannot ever go back into the old beliefs with the same conviction. Everything naturally unwinds, and there is greater sense of simply abiding in and as your natural state of presence-awareness. That is the whole enchilada in a nutshell, to mix metaphors.

# 6
## Keep Things Simple

*Question: I have continued to probe into this question of a 'reference point'. Not surprisingly, I cannot find one. Yet, suffering continues. It appears there are three difficulties I am having. First, in my current depressed state, when the pain being felt over a broken love affair is acute, there is a tendency for the mind to attempt to find the solution in the outside world. In particular, it seems that if I could win the girl back there would be instant relief. Seeing through the self center appears to be a more problematic solution at the moment. Of course, I can also ask, 'Who thinks it is more problematic?' I am sure this is not an original observation, but it seems overly simplistic for the nondualists to say, 'There is no distinction between you and me'. The fact is that I have a personal history, a visual perspective on the world, 'my' emotions, 'my' body and 'my' pain. Surely I am missing something fundamental in bringing up this point. Finally, a remaining hurdle for me is encapsulated in the following statement from your book 'Awakening to the Natural State': 'When you look deeply into this, you find that these ideas [of separation] never really touch you at all'.*

*Unless I am mistaken, the word 'you' is used in two different senses here. I assume that the 'you' that looks deeply is the thinking mind, because who else could be 'looking deeply'? Presumably not the presence-awareness, which has no ability to look. However, the 'you' that is never touched by ideas of separation is obviously presence-awareness, which is what you and I really are.*

*When I hear or read the verbal pointers, it is my mind that is trying to make sense of them. Perhaps it is even my mind that is trying to get out of its own way. It is a dog chasing its own tail. As you note, the answers cannot be found in the mind. But since we have no tools other than words to communicate this stuff, it seems to be an insolvable conundrum. You speak or write words, my thinking mind hears or reads and interprets words. Only the pointing finger is understood, not what is being pointed to. I think that is why people start talking about grace being required to 'get it', or there being nothing to 'get' at all.*

*I do not want to settle for a shabby kind of 'advaita-lite' experience. I do not want to feel somewhat better about myself because of my faith that ultimately everything is an appearance in presence-awareness, while meanwhile I have to read constantly to remind myself of that!*

John: I suggest you keep things simple and give up all the attempts to pin this down in thought. The questions you are asking appear cogent, but are not addressing the real issue. The real issue is your view of yourself. Everything spins from what you take yourself to be. This has nothing to do with advaita philosophy and pointers. After all, those are more words. You suffer because you take yourself to be what you are not. It is that simple.

Presence-awareness is here. It is clear and well-known at all times. No matter what you think, say or do, that natural presence, your real nature remains as the space in which all appears and disappears. It simply cannot be denied. You are and you know you are. In the absence of conceptualization based on the imagined person and its problems that awareness simply shines as a natural and open presence of clarity. This is known in direct experience. This is pointed out as a fact. If it is not clear, look into this and verify it for yourself. This part is already becoming clear for you at some level.

Forget all the double-speak and language analysis. In the end, that is simply looking into thought for an answer and away from the fact that what you are seeking is already fully present as your true nature. It is also failing to acknowledge that the mind alone is the cause of all your apparent doubts and problems. Keep things extremely practical. See how all psychological suffering (doubts, questions, problems, issues, dilemmas) is simply fabricated in thought. The truth is that all your questions and doubts are more of the same. As usual, our taking them seriously or believing in their reality draws us into the mind and the natural state is overlooked. We trade in the natural freedom of presence-awareness for self-centered thoughts. Unfortunately, the latter leads to doubt and suffering. For example, these questions are appearing, and you believe there is something valid in them. On the other hand, you could view them for what they ultimately are –thoughts floating in bright, clear, doubtless presence-awareness. And is there a problem with that?

Yet the tendency is to overlook this and go back to nursing the mind, attending to concepts and ideas and taking them seriously. You are jumping to the end game without fully investigating the steps along the way. To say that you know that there is no self, but that the suffering and problems are still arising, is too superficial. At a practical level of living this, it implies questioning everything you think and believe about yourself, all your supports and beliefs systems, all your ideas of what brings happiness and causes suffering.

*Q: Great suggestions. Even as I asked the questions, I felt like I was going further astray. Thank you for not compounding my error by addressing the questions directly. I am going to do some investigating to nail down the basics, as you say.*

John: Stick with the basics. Let the pointers continue to support your investigation into seeing what you are and what you are not. Once you are clear what your real nature is, then you can look back at the mind and question the habitual thoughts and assumptions that generate doubt and confusion. The basic understanding is there for you. All you need to do is apply what you know.

# 7

# Pain and Suffering

*Question: What about God? Is God in the pure conscious awareness that we are? Or are we an extension of a higher power? Can we turn to it for guidance in seeking a life partner? What about prayer? I have seen it heal. What happened there? What about how my heart hurts when I see all the suffering in the world, especially abandoned animals or children? What about pain in the body that arises? I still feel a sense of separation from God. This is driving my longing for a partner. I lost my Mother, Dad and a beloved Aunt over the past five years. It has been the 'dark night of the soul' dealing with their departures. How can I untangle myself from this? I still feel suffering.*

John: All questions, such as those you have raised, get resolved through understanding your true nature. The questions and doubts are created in the mind that imagines separation and believes that there is something wrong. That is all! With the dissolution of the belief in separation and the assumed defective, problematic self, all the questions are undercut.

God is another pointer to the one reality. Suffering arises from ignorance of who and what we are. The remedy is to get clear on the basics for yourself. Then you are in the best position to help others. You cannot fully help others without being clear on the basics. Physical pain arises or not. Who chooses it anyway? It is the self-centered story around the pain that generates suffering. That can be dealt with through applying the pointers. Pain and suffering are two separate issues. Use common sense to deal with pain to the extent possible. To resolve suffering understand what you are and what you are not.

[Follow up.]

Q: Thank you so much for this! After I sent you my emails, I could see the story in every single thing I wrote to you. I was talking about a fictional sense of 'me' who lost her parents and Aunt, who feels heartbroken at the world's cruelty to animals and children and so on. Damn, the pull of the story! And I know I have to see this for myself. Neither you nor anyone else can give this to me.

John: It is good that you are seeing how the story is made of thoughts centered around a fictional sense of 'I'. The first step in being free of thought is to see what is going on. You are getting the hang of this.

# 8
## Why Something Rather Than Nothing?

*Question: You asked me to keep you updated, but I have been remiss in that regard. So here goes. Basically, my word for it all is—wonderment. The shining shines like the sun, our cosmic origin. Call it miraculous, God, whatever. One basic question of philosophy is 'Why is there something rather than nothing?' At its deepest level the scientific model assumes an eventual explanation, which is an analogue for a box the world lives in. I am familiar with all the words, having read them many times. There is nowhere to go, nothing to do. An eighth of an inch difference and heaven and hell are split apart. It has all been said before, yet expresses nothing. All those words also involve boxes. Nothing, something. Something, nothing. Why? I do not know. It does not really matter anymore. The miracle, the wonderment goes on and on. My update is not very newsworthy, but there it is. The miraculous is no big deal.*

John: The question 'why something, rather than nothing?' is one of those seemingly cogent questions that disintegrates when examined. It is posed by the mind trying to get a grip on something which it can never understand. The mind appears in pure awareness and creates concepts of time, causality and separation and then tries to pin those concepts on that which is prior to the mind. How can the concepts of the mind apply to that which is before the mind ever was? It is the mind that says something has appeared over and against the primordial oneness. But that which has appeared is the same nature as its source. There is no separation, so there is no basis for the question. The question is false. Seeing this, the question drops, and you are left with what is. Call it ordinary, miraculous or anything you like. Those are only more labels.

*Q: Right you are. I listened to your broadcast with Allin Taylor, and in it you mention people who continue acquiring concepts. That hit me. They come to it and go right past it. I was one of them. Regarding your discussion about why something rather than nothing, that is clear. I had been confused by the presence-awareness. I assumed that it, too, had to disappear with death, but now I understand that it is a manifestation of the emptiness that keeps creating the world. I am that emptiness.*

John: You are that emptiness from which all things arise. That emptiness is not separate from pure awareness, because awareness is never cognized as an object. The emptiness and the awareness are one and the same. The non-objective emptiness that is your true nature is not an inert vacuum or void. That is the true emptiness. The things which appear are not different in essence from that either. How can they be, since they arise from it? This recognition cannot be grasped by the mind, yet it is directly known in immediate, non-conceptual seeing. It is the wordless, immediate recognition of that which is present and aware in you. You are that 'no thing' which cannot be grasped by the mind, but which undoubtedly is. Now you know! You can never lose your own being. It cannot be given or taken away. This is always present, closer than your next breath. It is already realized and recognized before the next thought appears.

# 9

# Awareness Is Not Knowable by the Mind

*Question: I wanted to ask about the point you make that enlightenment or knowledge of who we are is not a mental experience, nor does it have anything to do with the mind. I have read that countless times, but it meant something more to me this time. It felt like the knowledge of who we are is not a mental knowledge but an instinctive or formless knowledge, a kind of knowing without a need for an object of the knowing. This was helpful because it explains why we have the feeling of already understanding this completely, and yet at the same time not getting it. It is a weird conflict of understanding and confusion. It seems that this conflict continues as long as we hope that the understanding will move into a recognizable objective state where we can look at it and say 'yes, there it is, this is an enlightened state'.*

*If I stop and recall that this self-knowledge is not of or in the mind, that it is totally present and yet totally independent of the mind, then I can understand why there has been this sense of a permanent feeling of understanding ever since I can remember. In other words, I can see how understanding and confusion have been able to coexist, the confusion simply being a product of wanting to see the understanding in the mirror of the mind.*

John: The presence of awareness that is your real nature cannot be grasped or known by the mind. The mind is an appearance in awareness. It is an object of awareness. How can an object in awareness know the awareness that you are? Once you see this, you give up the attempt to understand this in the mind. Yet the fact of your true nature, as that which is present and aware, is easily recognized and noticed. In fact, such recognition is completely natural and effortless. As you mentioned, trying to understand your nature through the instrument of the mind results in confusion. This is because it cannot be done. Seeing this is an important insight.

## 10

# There Is No Need to Improve the Recognition

*Question: I find that you and others who talk about this say one particular thing that I get stuck on—that I cannot deny the very fact that I am aware and present.*

John: Good so far!

*Question: But I am not so sure that I am! When I ask, 'Who is it that says I am not?' or 'Who is it that doubts?' I get stuck in a mire.*

John: At that point, you miss the simplicity of things and step back into the mind. You are moving from the fact of presence-awareness, which is undeniable, and stepping back into the mind to try to 'improve' the recognition. But if you see the radical point that the answer cannot be known, recognized or grasped by the mind, you will not go there. You do not look for water in a mirage, once you see it as a mirage.

*Q: I am not sure what an 'I' is. Using the word seems to direct me back to what I mentally think of as a 'me', that is, the body-mind organism. So asking 'who?' or 'what?' becomes a circle.*

John: 'I' is only a word, a concept, a label in the mind. At best it is a pointer back to your true nature. You are the undeniable knowingness that is aware of that thought and all else. This is so utterly simple that we often miss the basic point. If there is some residual belief in your identity as being limited to the body-mind, then look at that to see if it is really true. You are that space of knowing presence in which the body, mind and world appear and disappear. This is not a mystical understanding but a simple fact you can see with a bit of looking. Remember, this in not a philosophical or speculative endeavor. Your being is not a speculation. There is nothing conceptual about it.

*Question: Sometimes I feel tuned into the natural state. But isn't it really a non-state?*

John: 'State' and 'non-state' are only words. Who or what is knowing those concepts? There are any number of pointers. None of them are right or wrong in themselves. Find one that resonates and follow it back to the fact of your true nature.

*Question: The word 'I' seems very coarse and ugly, and I get stuck by using it.*

John: Knowing what you are has nothing to do with words. So either forget the words or simply see that they are provisional pointers. If you look back to words and thoughts, what I am pointing out will seem mysterious. However, this is only due to looking in the wrong direction.

*Question: Is this mental confusion created because anything other than 'I' is unknown and because the mind can only cope with an entity?*

John: It comes from looking for an answer in the mind, where it can never be found. Your true nature is to be known, recognized or acknowledged non-conceptually, without reference to thought or anything else. Your true nature is not in the mind and cannot be grasped by the mind. You cannot eat spaghetti with a pitchfork, so do not try!

*Question: Aren't I supposed to always know the truth of my being?*

John: You are present and aware. This is undeniable. It is a fact that cannot be refuted. It is not to be known or sought as if it is some special object or state. It is the ever-present basis of all experiences. How many thoughts can you have without the presence of awareness? It is so evident that is does not even need to be known, really. It is pointed out and simply acknowledged. Without thinking, seeking or finding, you are that.

# Handling Doubts and Confusion

*Question: Things are settling in since our meeting. The negation of what appears in the awareness was what I had been pursuing. But as you said, it was looking in the wrong direction and the focus was on the objects. Now when I ask 'Am I aware?' there is no effort necessary. It is instantaneous, because it was never lost! How simple it is to ignore this! I do not need to do anything to see this. Making an effort means that I think I am separate from awareness, which further strengthens the belief in the separate 'I'. What I observed was that the feeling of 'I', as pointed to by Nisargadatta Maharaj, is the same as what is pointed to by this 'Am I aware?' question. It is very easy and effortless. The interesting thing is you do not even need to ask 'Am I aware?' If any confusion arises, it arises in this awareness. I will let it settle and keep you posted about the progress. What progress!? Thank you very much!*

John: Your insights are good. They are consistent with the basic pointers I was sharing. Continue to notice that the recognition of your true nature is direct and immediate. See that in direct investigation no separate person can be found apart from this. This looking will demolish any residual questions and doubts. As you correctly state, any doubt or confusion must appear in awareness. You are that. In all times, places and situations you are that undeniable presence of awareness that is beyond doubt.

## 12

# Life Finds Its Natural Expression

*Question: I was led to this recently after years of passionate and joyful spiritual study. Then, suddenly, after a meditation seminar, desires began to drop away. I literally could not meditate anymore. The searching waned, then stopped! I did not understand what was happening. I began to search for answers and was led to the pointers that you so wonderfully express, among others. What a surprise, I was definitely not looking for this. It is proof that I am being lived, that I had no choice, that what is happening is simply happening.*

*So, here I am. And that is it! It is amazing and confusing and ordinary, and I do not know what else. There are many states that pass through lately. The shining presence is always there. I am cooking, being fried up, baking in the oven, being marinated and barbecued! I do not have any ambitions anymore. I hardly have any desires either. I want to quit my job, which I wanted to do even before all this. I have no interest in getting another one for the time being. I just want to be, you know? I know that this will change. Is this typical? Have you ever heard of this total lack of desire to do or create? I used to love to write, but I have not written anything in months. There is no interest whatsoever! I mean, I am here. I love this life. I am grateful and curious. There is a passion, curiosity and love for life happening. But there is no need or desire to do anything with this life. Now I see that I never was in control anyway.*

John: Knowing who are you does not mean you will sit on a rock and do nothing. The natural life and intelligence that you are finds its natural expression. It has been living your life all along and will continue to do so. Whatever you do or do not do, you can never leave the presence that you are. The creating and doing that was motivated from the position of being a limited, separate self can fall away through lack of any continued interest. Then you will have to see what comes up naturally to do outside of that belief system. As long as the body and mind are there, something will come up to be done! You will have to see what that will be. And do not forget, there is no separate doer in the picture anyway, so who is doing what?

[Follow up]

Q: *Thank you for responding. This is very clear. It is a different way of being, one that I truly welcome. I have no idea where I will be moved, but also no doubt that all is happening as it should. This is such a comforting realization. A deep knowingness of well-being arises.*

## 13

# There Is No One

*Question: Here I am, writing to you so soon. I had a very emotional day yesterday. What is coming up right now is to just stop. There is a deep desire to stop all trying, hoping, wondering, controlling and doubting. I see that nothing I have ever done has made a bit of difference in what was supposed to happen. It is happening through me, as me! But the thought is that if I let go and stop trying to mold this life into something, all hell will break loose and everything will fall apart. As if 'I' were holding it together in the first place! This is so laughable now. Life will go on as it always has! This is a little mind-blowing and, I must say, a great relief. I simply cannot convince myself that 'I' have anything to do with what happens in this life. God, this is liberating! The thought was that nothing would happen if no effort were applied or no direction were chosen. But it is so silly, isn't it? Who is in charge anyway? This is so humbling.*

John: At the risk of stating what has become clear to you—there is no one. The radical message of 'no one' means that there is no entity to let go, stop, drop or do anything whatsoever. There is a seeing that there is no one present at all apart from the obvious presence-awareness that cannot be denied. All that appears is an expression or manifestation within that. Nothing is added, nothing is lost. There is no individual person, entity, doer, decider, chooser, thinker or independent being. This understanding immediately severs all questions, doubts, problems and psychological suffering—which are all predicated on the existence of a separate one who owns all that. That is the master sword stroke. Any doubt or worry is only a concept appearing in the clear awareness that you are. Nothing can touch 'no thing'.

You do not need me or anyone to confirm the recognition of what you are and what you are not. It is all there in clear view in immediate seeing. All anyone can do is point. The seeing and understanding are your own. Once you see this, any book or person can only point to what you already know.

*Q: This hit me between the eyes! There is stunned silence. Are you saying that there is no body-mind 'puppet' being lived? That the body-mind is not real? It is only an appearance in the awareness? If so, everything is an appearance in the awareness. There are no actual entities. Is this what you are pointing to?*

John: Yes. You are that obvious presence-awareness that cannot be denied. It is not an attainment, understanding or achievement. Because that is what you are, there is no approach to it. Nor is there a deepening or stabilization. It is a matter of identity. There is nothing to do with a fact of identity. All is done now, here, today. You are what you are seeking. All else is only an appearance in this that you are. An appearance is something with no independent or substantial nature at all. It does not truly exist. It only appears to be. What are appearances? They are movements, vibrations, waves appearing—in and on what? On your nature of pure, non-objective awareness. Are waves something other than the water on which they appear? There is no separation from the source. It is all one substance.

Awareness, your real being is all there is. You are that, and there is only that. There are no puppets, no entities, no understandings and no one present to stop trying. All is an imagined appearance, a passing ripple on the expanse of the pure ocean of awareness, which is 'no thing'. You are that 'no thing'. 'No thing' needs nothing. That 'no thing' is full to perfection. You are that.

Today, now, as this is being read, all is done. All is complete. The dream of separation is over. There has never, ever been a separation from that. This resolves all doubts and questions. It immediately annihilates the seeking and suffering, for those are based on a separation from oneness, which is seen never to have occurred. The cause of suffering is investigated and found to be absent. What remains is all there ever was—pure, space-like, shining, clear, wordless presence-awareness. It takes no effort to be. You are already what you are seeking.

## 14
# Past and Future Are Present Ideas

*Question: Thank you very much for your response to my email about self-knowledge being entirely outside of the mind. I want to ask you about 'newness'. For me, this feeling of newness is important. There has been a sense that every experience, including every thought, is completely new and has never occurred before. Driving along a familiar road today, it seemed that, in a certain way, I had never seen this road before, that I did not know it at all. On a basic level, I have driven along this road many times, but on a more fundamental level, it was a completely new experience. It is a feeling that there is no joining between experiences. If I look closely at things, particularly my thoughts, they take on a feeling of being completely new and magically fresh. As such, they have no concurrent feeling of being restrictive or painful. Can you comment on this?*

John: I agree. Each thought, feeling, experience or occurrence arises fresh and new in each moment. Past and future themselves are present ideas arising in the fresh moment of now. Awareness, your true nature, is timeless, because time is a creation of thought. Without thought there is no time at all. So time arises in the mind, but awareness stands beyond in a different realm altogether. Whether thoughts appear or not, you remain as you are.

Taking ourselves to be an entity in the appearance, a separate 'I' apart from pure presence-awareness, is the root concept to be seen through. Once that notion arises, the seeming entity gets caught in the apparent past and future. It searches for wholeness and freedom in time, which is purely conceptual. In this process, the natural presence of awareness, which is what we are, is overlooked.

Questioning the concept of time greatly undercuts the underpinnings of the imaginary separate self. In direct perception, or immediate looking, there is no time, nor any separate self. There is only the undeniable presence of awareness that you are. Seeing this is immediate freedom. No process or time is involved. Time is not real, so how could a reliance on time lead to the recognition of the timeless presence that you are?

# 15
## Investigating the Mind

*Question: I am in Canada. If you know of anyone who speaks about this kind of thing up here, I would love to know about it. But I doubt there is anyone out here!*

John: I cannot say I have any friends up in your area to refer you to. The good news is that you have everything you need with you. The undeniable sense presence of awareness that is with you right now is all that this is about. You are that. This cannot be denied. There is really nothing more to know than this.

All that might be left is dealing with the mind. What is the mind that we are concerned with? It is all the residual habits, doubts, beliefs and fears that attract our interest. In following those ideas, we overlook the fact that as that presence-awareness, we are already free. It is good to understand at a gut level that, in terms of self-knowledge, there is no real answer of any consequence in the mind. If you can see this, then look away from the mind and pay it no attention. If you do not attend to or grasp self-defining thoughts, then there is nothing to do, fix or know. Thoughts simply pass through, leaving you as you are—present and aware. This is the essence of abiding in freedom.

In years past, we imagined ourselves to be separate—a person, a limited individual. With this concept came separation, loneliness, doubt and fear. Then the mind went off on quest, gathering all types of identifications and beliefs to fix this apparent problem. But it never really worked because the root assumption was not true. Self-centered problems and suffering are only due to thoughts and ideas picked up in the years of ignorance. Once you understand what is happening, how all the trouble arises from unexamined beliefs based on a false premise, a natural sense of questioning comes in. The fixation on and attachment to the mind and its contents rapidly wanes. What keeps us interested in the mind is the belief that what it is saying is true. A little bit of investigation is enough to undermine the whole house of cards.

No matter what the mind thinks, says, or does it is only an appearance in the bright, clear presence of your true nature. That remains unaffected at all times. Simply recognize this. The natural clarity and joy that comes up will make you less and less inclined to run after thoughts, which only leads to doubt and suffering. As far as I am concerned, the mind must be investigated and understood. Otherwise, we will always be in the grip of thoughts, which we still believe and take to be real.

*Q: Right now it is all crystal clear. It is hard to believe it could ever be obscured. But I have been 'back and forth' enough times to know that it does seem to be as you are describing.*

John: The 'back and forth' experience is an optical illusion, so to speak. Thoughts come and go in present awareness, which is always shining. Even when thoughts are not happening, there is a recognition that thoughts are not happening. This is so simple that we overlook the obvious. Not seeing this, the focus drifts onto the story line or content in thought. We pay more attention to the thoughts than the awareness and then say that the awareness has gone away. But has it? How can you even be aware of thoughts if there is no awareness present? This gets pointed out and you stop for a moment and notice the obvious. Once you see this, 'getting it and losing it' is not possible. You cannot move away from what you are.

Thoughts coming and going is not problem because they all appear and disappear in present awareness. You are not a separate self apart from the reality, which is your true nature, which is present and brightly aware. Seeing this, the ego-notion, or belief in individuality, is undercut. The root of all doubts and suffering is removed. What remains is a life in clarity—a clarity that cannot leave because it is what you are. You cannot lose yourself under any circumstances. By looking this way, you immediately come into the recognition of what you are. Here, recognizing means simply being what you are and have always been. This is the essence of what is pointed out. Continue to look into this until it is clear and beyond doubt. Reality is always closer than your next thought, because each and every thought arises in inescapable present awareness.

## 16

# It Is Done

*Question: It is done! There is only awareness, not a person. This makes all the talk of the process of 'getting it' meaningless. More than meaningless—there is nothing there! There is only awareness! There is no time involved. God! I am sounding like you now, but I get it. All it took was for you to point me back to the obvious. There are no layers, rewiring or increments. That was all a fiction. There is only awareness, and anything else is a story. All of that stuff is just a fiction –it never was. All of what I was insisting was real, all the processing and unfolding, is not real. There was an 'I' trying to hold onto a pleasant experience, trying to quantify it and make a mental model of it. That had me enslaved to a thinking self and blind to the true nature of awareness. There was a whole story about that. But for whom did the story exist? And who cares? There is nothing there. It is gone—poof! There is just the awareness that has always been here! There has never been anything like an asleep person or an awake person. There is nothing here but awareness now.*

*I see now that what you pointed out to me that first night—and what I saw for myself a few days later—is all. At the time, I saw that it was true, but I did not get that it was all. That is the piece that is here now. There is nothing but that. Thank you!*

John: There is some good seeing shining through there! Remember that because awareness is all— that you are that and have never been separate from that—it is not a matter of being done, but only seeing the ever-present facts that were only overlooked. Sometimes people get into a 'now I am done, now I am not' mode, which can be a cycle. This is because there is a subtle reference to the 'I' that is done, then not done. The clear seeing of the truth that there is no person cuts the conceptual loop. Freedom is never in time, but always in the immediate recognition of present, undeniable being-awareness, your true nature.

There is nothing wrong with questions or experiences coming up. Come back to the fact of present freedom and question any contrary concepts. The answer is here in plain view and ever present. Everything else is an unfounded concept.

# 17

## Things Are Free to Flow

*Question: Ramana Maharshi used to say 'Be as you are'. Nisargadatta Maharaj advised people to stay in the 'I am'. I did not understand what they meant until now. Of course, as you make clear, even your own descriptions, such as 'presence-awareness' and the 'natural state', can only be pointers to something ultimately indefinable. There is no need to get hung up on the words.*

*There is no doubt that the reason why I, like you and so many others, overlooked this for so long, is that it is so simple and obvious. I must have had innumerable moments of thought-free 'presence-awareness' in my life, but I never thought that they were in any way special or significant, which of course they are not, really. They are just our 'natural state'. After I first 'got it', a few weeks ago, I tried to make efforts at times to stay in this state. In practice, this amounted to turning away from thoughts as soon as I realized that I had been thinking. But I now realize that this was mistaken. As you say, our natural state never leaves us, whether it is overlaid by thinking or not. Any kind of practice brings a subtle reinforcement of the sense of 'I'. It seems that, as you suggest, thoughts gradually diminish of themselves as they are starved of the customary interest we have shown them. I find that this is already starting to happen, in fact.*

*The other side of the coin, of course, is the removal of the false ideas that I have had about myself. I had been attracted to the practice of self-inquiry ever since I discovered Ramana Maharshi some thirty years ago. However, it appeared to me, at the time, to be a rigorous and very demanding discipline, ideally involving years of living with a guru in an ashram in India. I did not feel able to desert my already elderly parents or my full-time career as a lawyer. I retired from work in 2003, both my parents having meanwhile died.*

*However, I had by then started reading some of the modern non-duality literature, and I had begun to wonder whether the pilgrimage to India was really necessary.*

*I had long since been intellectually persuaded that 'I' was not the body, thoughts, emotions, sensations or anything else that I could think of. But I had still thought that there needed to be some kind of further, sustained self-inquiry beyond that. What I had not realized is that the 'I' is simply a fictitious thought. It does not exist. Mind you, given a lifetime's conditioning to believe that I was a person (in fact, a body), it takes some time for that conditioning to be removed. I find that constant self-reminders are needed. I sense your objection to this: I am introducing the concept of time, which is an illusion. I am again prepared to accept intellectually that time and space, like the ego, are mental illusions. But unless one is in a permanent state of 'nirvikalpa samadhi', it seems that in practice one has to live with them! I have some reservations about your statement that 'there are no levels of awareness', but I do not think that it would help to get involved in a debate about that. I am sure that you have no desire to do so, either!*

*I do have one question. As you will have gathered from the above, I am quite an intellectual type, given to much thinking. However, many non-duality teachers, including Ramana Maharshi and Nisargadatta Maharaj, indicate that thinking is not our natural state. Maharaj actually speaks of allowing the mind to 'fast' or 'be starved'. I will certainly be doing less reading from now on, spiritual or otherwise, because the search is essentially over. But, as a pastime, I like doing puzzles, for example, crosswords, Sudoku, chess problems and so on. Do you think it would help me to give up those, too? It would not be difficult for me to do so because I am not addicted to them.*

John: Thank you for the detailed and heart-felt letter. I am glad to hear that the pointers have resonated and played a part to confirm your own direct experience of 'the natural state', which is shining constantly and always as the presence-awareness that cannot be denied. Ramana Maharshi used to say that each one is already the Self, and being the Self, there is no need for any realization as such. That is what I call the positive side of the coin—the revelation of what is real, our true nature, which is shining in plain view right from the start. The dissolution of seeking and suffering through self-inquiry is a very practical approach to tackle any residual doubts and questions in the mind by tracing them to the assumed 'I thought' or self-center. This investigation shows that the root thought or conceptual core of all the imagined bondage cannot be found. Simply put, there is no separate individual who is the recipient of all the false, self-centered concepts. In this way, you discover that all doubts, questions, problems and dilemmas are in relation to a reference point, the 'I', which is itself an unexamined concept.

As far as mental pursuits or other interests—no activity or undertaking of the body-mind can present a conflict with the recognition of your true nature. To try to manipulate the appearance and artificially repress or indulge in activities would only be in reference to some conceptual position by an individual with some goal in mind. There is no goal because you are already what you seek. From this seeing there is only the spontaneous arising of thoughts, feelings and activities from moment to moment. Let the body-mind live out its expression in whatever way appears natural to it. When not encumbered by conceptual, self-centered thought, things are free to flow and a natural intelligence and compassion are there. Blueprints, plans and regimens are for the imagined, defective self who thinks it must do something special to be 'right'. However, as you now know, there is no person at all. You are already home—as that self-shining, presence-awareness that you cannot leave, even if you try.

# One Substance

*Question: There have been a number of insights I wanted to share with you. The most remarkable one is that absolutely all seems to be made of awareness or consciousness. Everything.*

John: This sounds like pure non-duality to me. There are not too many places to go or problems to have when all is just one substance!

*Q: When I look into present direct experience, I cannot find any tangible object or experience I can call the mind or the world. What can be seen is a number of interrelated functions taking place in a timeless and dimensionless backdrop. There are thoughts but nothing that can be called a mind. The container of thought is empty, timeless consciousness itself. The mind as an object exists only when conceptualized.*

John: This is very clear.

*Q: The same applies to the body. It does not exist as a static object. The experience of a body is the result of the operation of the senses in the moment. Input from the senses gathered into consciousness from moment to moment makes the 'body'. Even the notion of a succession of moments does not exist in reality. It is a notion only. The body as an object exists only when conceptualized.*

John: Yes.

*Q: What is also clear is that there are definite realms in the manifested consciousness. One is the senses and their physical/percep-*

tual/sensorial experiences. Another is subtler and is emotional and connects sentient beings. This realm accounts for my feeling that 'John', as a sentient being exists even though we are not in the immediate reach of one another's senses. It is a feeling of another's presence as a creature. Then there is the mental realm which is equal to imagery, conceptualization and language.

John: Anything may arise in the appearance, and yet it is all an appearance of the one non-dual presence. The difference is in the appearance, but in essence it is all the oneness itself appearing in those forms.

Q: The world is nothing but a combination of experience in these three realms, with an emphasis on one or another. The world is entirely created in consciousness. The world is the experience of the world. The world as an object or collection of objects exists only when conceptualized.

John: Extremely clear!

Q: In the same manner, 'I' cannot be found as an object. 'I' as an object exists only when conceptualized. There is only the stuff described above and emptiness, emptiness, emptiness—alert and full-of-life emptiness. In view of all this, the notion of or desire for enlightenment is absent. When it pops back up in consciousness, like everything else, it is seen for what it is.

John: All desire or seeking is motivated by a belief that there is something with a substantial, independent existence. But nothing really exists apart from the 'alert and full-of-life emptiness', as you call it. Then the mind alights upon no concept whatsoever. Seeing this, there is peace.

## 19
## Clarity Does Not Come and Go

*Question: Last week there was a very deep and obvious recognition of this presence-awareness. It was immediate, simple and undeniable.*

John: This is so simple that we can overlook what is being pointed to. Presence-awareness is happening always. Weren't you present and aware all week? This is not an experience, but the background of any and all experiences.

*Question: Shortly after, things happened and I was swamped with thoughts, intense emotions and issues that I thought were resolved. It seemed that I was unaware of my true nature during this time! I was completely in the drama and emotions.*

John: It is only the focus of attention going to some old habits. But did you stop being present or aware? There is nothing wrong with thoughts going through. Besides, you cannot stop them anyway. However, if there is belief in them they seem attractive. If not, they float through effortlessly.

*Question: They had their way with me, so to speak. Then yesterday, suddenly it was over. Peace and clarity are here again. I remember again who I really am. Whatever that means!*

John: The clarity does not come and go. It is not a state. It is the light of pure presence that is illuminating and supporting all thoughts, ideas and feelings. When we get wrapped up in thought we overlook that awareness is what is present and knowing the thoughts!

*Question: I was so identified as a person with feelings, needs and thoughts! I knew that I was much more, but I was not experiencing that in my day-to-day living. Do you know what I mean?*

John: Interest in thoughts and concepts means being interested or captivated by thoughts of a separate self. That goes on as long as there is some residual belief that there is such a self. Once you see that the separate self is a complete fiction, the root of self-centered thought is severed.

*Question: I am not even going to ask if this will ever be a day-to-day reality. It is what it is, no matter what I think. I know it is useless to think that the awareness comes in and out of my experience.*

John: Verify that it does not come and go. There can be no wavering in and out of something that is always present.

*Question: Is this also something you still experience after recognizing the truth, I mean being really 'in' those feelings and thoughts?*

John: You cannot be in feelings and thoughts. You are that awareness that knows them. They are in you. The residual interest in them goes on as long the core belief in the existence of the separate 'I' has any momentum. What keeps us interested in thoughts and feelings is the belief that they are true and that they say something real about who we are. But do they? They are all about an assumed sense of self. Did you find any actual thing that is the seeming self? Seeing this mechanism through to the core unwinds the whole production. Seeing your true nature of present awareness is key, but also key is seeing that all concepts are built on a self that cannot be found. This dismantles the belief and interest in self-centered thought.

## 20
## The Answer Is Not in the Mind

*Question: You wrote: 'Seeing this mechanism through to the core unwinds the whole production. Seeing your true nature of present awareness is key, but also key is seeing that all concepts are built on a self that cannot be found. This dismantles the belief and interest in self-centered thought'. I want to see the mechanism through to the core, like you said, but is there really anything I can do about this? Because I do not really exist, 'I' have no control over this, do I?*

John: Set aside the approach of 'I do not exist, so what can I do?'. That is only conceptual at this point. If you truly believed there was nobody there, there would be no one to suffer, to ask a question and so on. We would not be having this dialogue! That is a trap that many fall into. Also, the 'I have no control' statement misses the point. It leads to unclear seeing and passivity. I have never seen anyone making any real headway laboring under these concepts. They are often asserted without a depth of understanding of the meaning of the words. See the basics for yourself and be done with spinning in the mind!

*Q: I guess I am struggling with the reality that I already am 'that'.*

John: You know that you are. This is beyond doubt. Stop there and be. Start to think of what that means and you step back into thought and doubt. The answer is not in the mind. You are and you know that you are. Do not move from this. Do not conceptualize it. First make sure that the fact of your being as present awareness is clear. We can get into what it means later. First of all you have to see what is being pointed out. If you keep jumping back to the mind, you miss the immediate and non-conceptual recognition of this. You are and you know you are. Is this clear? Do not think! See this, know this, feel this without conceptualizing this simple fact.

*Q: My daily experience seems to be as a separate person. Any suggestions? Should I stop thinking about it? Should I question the concept of a separate self?*

John: First and foremost see that all problems, doubts, seeking and questions are only creations in thought. You cannot stop thinking. Who would want to? What you need to do is see what is occurring. At this point, you are jumping at every passing thought and doubt in the mind, assuming it to be a cogent issue. The first step in approaching the mind is to see, really see, that all these issues are passing thoughts. Apart from thoughts, where are these issues? Once you see that these are only thoughts, not realities, you are in a position to question whether what the thoughts are saying is even true or not.

If these points are not clear, you will keep overlooking your true nature and continue clutching at every random passing thought. The mind will lead you around like a bull being lead by a ring through its nose. Why? Because you do not know what you are and you will take everything the mind says about you to be true. You undoubtedly are present and aware. Every problem, doubt and issue is nothing but a thought. Seeing this will dismantle the roots of suffering. See what you come up with.

# 21
# Mental Activity Versus Self-Centered Thinking

*Question: So far as mental pursuits are concerned, what you say is entirely logical and consistent. Mental pursuits of the kind to which I referred in a previous email (for example, doing crossword puzzles) are really only 'self-centered' in the sense that, obviously, it is 'I' who am pursuing them.*

John: Not really. They are just happening. They are impersonal activities. They are not self-centered unless they are referenced to the imagined separate self. If not, they go on quite impersonally, with no sense of psychological bondage.

*Q: I see that they are not self-centered in the sense of being related to gaining an imagined future advantage of some kind, because the only goal involved is the solution of the puzzle. When that is achieved, the puzzle can be forgotten about.*

John: This activity is totally benign! The universe, including 'your' body is an endless stream of unceasing activity. You cannot stop it, even if you want to. There is no personal 'self' involved at all.

*Q: The following may possibly amuse you. On Saturday, I was slightly depressed by the thought that there was no practice that I could follow to help bring about the desired state of permanent happiness.*

John: There is no need to seek for this. Present awareness is already here. You are that, and there is nothing else needed. Drop the concept that it is not here!

Q: *Shortly before going to bed, I realized that it was foolish to think like that. Who is there to be depressed, anyhow?*

John: Good. See that as a passing thought. If believed in, there are subsequent thoughts and emotions based on the assumed reality of it. If it is not believed, there is ever-present, natural ease.

Q: *The question seemed to remain, however, of how I was to spend my time for the rest of my life. It was at least a minute before I realized that I had again fallen into the same trap! There is no 'I' whose time has to be spent, nor, indeed, do 'I' have any life of my own to lead!*

John: Excellent, you saw the trap this time.

Q: *As you so rightly say, all 'I' can do is 'let the body-mind live out its expression in whatever way appears natural to it'.*

John: Get the 'I' completely out of the picture. Now! There is no 'I'. There is only spontaneous appearing and functioning. There is no 'I' to 'let' or 'not let'. There is only what is appearing right here, right now in present awareness.

Q: *It is not too clear, at present, but we shall see.*

John: Set aside conceptual thoughts, assumptions and reference points and see the natural state. There is only pure presence-awareness and the spontaneously display of activity that comes up.

Q: *Following the same line of thought, it seems that there is really nothing more to say, for who is there to say it?*

John: Ultimately, true. But as long as that appearance of a

body-mind is there, actions and speech will likely arise!

Q: *Possibly the time may come when this body-mind mechanism may be able to experience and communicate thoughts spontaneously.*

John: And how are they going on right now? Are you choosing the next thought or action? Or are they happening spontaneously? Remember, nothing new needs to be brought in. It is only seeing clearly what is and has always been the case. Previously, we saw 'what is' through a distorting lens of erroneous concepts.

Q: *Perhaps silence is golden?*

John: Talking or not, you cannot deny the fact of your present awareness. You are that whether you talk or not, even whether you know it or not!

Q: *Best wishes. Though from whom to whom?*

John: From you to me. But that 'you' and 'me' are not different in essence. You cannot get away from oneness!

[Follow up.]

Question: *Thank you very much for your detailed comments on my last email. My initial reaction is that I can understand and accept all your responses, except the one saying that I do, already, experience and communicate thoughts spontaneously. My communications, in particular, have always been quite considered, especially written ones (due to the desire to express myself precisely). In my career as a lawyer, it would have been very dangerous to give spontaneous replies to questions! I feel that I am perhaps missing the point here? I do appreciate your continuing help.*

John: Look to see if the next thought that comes up is calculated in advance or spontaneously appears. This is one way to see that there is no person or entity in the picture. Thoughts are spontaneous occurrences. Even the thought 'I must be careful and not say anything out of order' is a spontaneous appearance. It is not by, for or about someone. It is simply appearing on the screen of awareness. There is awareness and thoughts arising. There is no one or nothing else in the picture. Least of all is there a 'you' in the works at all, except as an assumption.

## Focusing on Thoughts

*Question: I have difficulty feeling the serenity.*

John: This is not about feeling serenity. When there is natural resting as presence-awareness and the focus is off of conceptual thought, there is a natural peace and everything is perfectly fine as is. There is no special state that needs to be imported. Nor is this implying that there is an absence of thinking, feeling or any other activity. Those all go on quite effortlessly.

*Q: I notice that I often think about ego-inflating stories, in order to feel good.*

John: Yes, but does this really work and is it needed? Following the mind in order to feel good is the age-old pursuit. You have to determine if it really works and is sustainable. In the end you see that thoughts are simply appearing and disappearing of themselves. You are not creating them. Nor is there any 'you' present. It is the belief in the 'I' that is the real joker in the pack, not the thoughts themselves.

*Q: Today, I went over the pointers from your meetings and saw how what I have been doing is focusing on thoughts.*

John: We return to the activities or thoughts in an effort to find peace or happiness. But is that really where happiness lies? Some careful looking may be helpful. If we happen to find the lasting answer by believing the thoughts, fine. The question is, though, did we really find it? Does that approach really work? Part of the motivation for clear seeing comes from the recognition that the past approaches may not have worked so well. If we still think they work, we may not have much motivation to see the pointers. Why do so, if we feel we already have access to happiness?

Q: *As you said, it does not matter so much about the thoughts. They are movements in the awareness.*

John: This is very simple, but true.

Q: *My question was not so much about trying not to think, but about how to focus on the awareness rather than always obsessively trying to entertain my mind. Of course, we cannot focus on awareness, for it is not an object. I think that un-focusing a bit from the thoughts and sensations would be helpful!*

John: Excellent insight. But you cannot 'unfocus from thoughts' by an act of will. That is another thought! It is better to simply see what is happening. Focus or unfocusing are at the mental level. That does not get to the roots of the matter. We focus on thought because we are interested in it. Why? What is it about thought that interests us? And is this interest leading to the understanding we are hoping for? This is inquiring at a deeper level, rather than at the surface of things. As long as there is residual belief in thoughts or the prospect of happiness in them, we return to them.

Q: *When I think of Nisargadatta Maharaj and his advice to hold on to the sense of being, that helps. Have you anything to add?*

John: Realize that the natural state is always present. It is not a matter of focusing on it. It is a fact that cannot be denied. The belief that the answers are available in the mind keeps us going back for more! But if we can see that the answer is really not there, we begin to lose interest in thought, and the understanding opens up. There is a sense of a relaxation into the clear presence of pure, non-conceptual knowing. It is so sweet and clear, like fresh water to a thirsty traveler. As this source is recognized, there is a natural desire to remain with that, rather then to follow dry, empty thoughts.

## 23

# Presence-Awareness Needs No Help

*Question: I emailed you sometime ago, and I thank you for your responses. But I need help again.*

John: Pure presence-awareness always is. It needs no help because it is the foundation of everything that is. However, if we believe ourselves to be apart from that, the mind conjures up the notion of the separate 'I' and the sense of wholeness seems to be divided. But the separation is only an appearance due to a misunderstanding. The remedy, as always, is to come back and see the basic facts of who and what we really are, as opposed to what the mind is telling us about ourselves.

*Q: I seem to be experiencing cycles. One week I feel strongly aware of my being as presence; the next week I feel lost in thought.*

John: This is due to some residual belief in the validity of self-referencing concepts. Once this is thoroughly questioned, the belief is snapped and you get out of the mental spin cycle.

*Q: I am not sure what triggers the recognition of my nature. For example, I may read the same pointers. Sometimes they work, sometimes not.*

John: There are likely a few concepts or beliefs not fully seen. It is hard to get to the core of this in email. It is quicker and easier to talk in person and cut through to the real issues. I have gone over the basic mechanism of the origins and roots of suffering and what keeps it alive in my writings. Have you seen that material? If not, check it out. Or we can talk in person.

Q: *I wonder if you could tell me what has changed for you? Is it that, instead of looking for yourself as something in the mind, you constantly see that your presence is not locatable there, yet can be felt always?*

John: Yes. Ultimately, this is what it comes down to. The fact is that your present awareness, which is what you are, is not confined or contained in thought, even now. It stands above and beyond and completely untouched. That is a fact. It is pointed out and seen to be so. It is the residual interest in thought that keeps us from seeing the obvious.

Q: *Although I can sometimes feel myself as being this 'no thing' in which all things appear, this sense of presence, I can never feel myself as awareness.*

John: There is no need to feel it. Feeling is a dualistic experience. You do not feel awareness. Feelings arise in awareness. If you try to feel it, you will get tied up.

Q: *How can I bring about the realization that I am awareness?*

John: Ask yourself if you are present and aware. The answer must be yes. That recognition is the seeing. This is undeniable and certain. Be willing to stick on that point and linger for a bit.

Q: *How can I feel the truth of it?*

John: Here you are stepping back into the mind, looking for something that you think you do not have. The simplicity of being present awareness is overlooked and traded in for some idea of what we think it should be. See this fallacy.

Q: *I am gradually more able to be aware of myself as presence. I am no further on the path of realizing myself as awareness.*

John: But you are aware, are you not? This presence that you are, is it dead, void, inert? Are you not only present but also aware? Aren't you knowing all thoughts, feelings and sensations? You say 'I am aware of myself as a presence'. That is the awareness itself in action. Presence and awareness are just pointers to the same wordless fact of your true nature.

The reason this appears difficult is because what you are is not an object. Sometimes it is called 'emptiness', but it is not a vacuum or a void. It is simultaneously present and cognizant. You cannot grasp it and try to pin it down as some thing, some feeling, some experience. If you do, you will overlook the simplicity of this. Relax and acknowledge the undeniable fact of presence, which is clear and brightly aware in you. Release your focus on the mind and conceptual thought. Relax the attempt to find something that is not present. Relax in the direct knowing of pure presence-awareness. Be willing to see what that seeing naturally reveals.

Q: *Your help is greatly appreciated. I do not like to sound so melodramatic, but I truly am sick of the search.*

John: Good! Because the search is useless. You already are what you seek. You do not fully see this nor trust your experience—yet. But you will.

Q: *I know I am what I am seeking, but I cannot feel it.*

John: This is a useless impasse. Do not try to feel it. That will turn presence-awareness into an object, which it cannot be. Out of habit, you are continuing to search, but the search is now useless because the answer is present and shining in direct experience. Do not try to conceptualize it or build it up into an experience. Your true nature is not a feeling! Leave off all the judgment and thinking. Be with this without turning it into a concept or imagining it as an experience.

Q: *I am bored of seemingly being this pseudo-entity. I want to go home, which I painfully realize I already am!*

John: You are present and aware. This is recognized in immediate knowing. Apart from a few random thoughts, feelings or sensations passing through, did you ever find anything that could be a substantial entity at all? If it is not there, how can you be such a thing? The belief in an entity goes on because we think it is there. It needs to be questioned a bit. Then all the belief and concern drops out of the picture.

Q: *How can it be so hard to know what I am?*

John: It is not hard. You already know what you are. You are still following a few concepts in the mind and giving them belief. Ideas are ideas. In non-conceptual understanding of what you are, they are worthless. What are ideas but some ripples floating through the undeniable presence-awareness that you are? See this clearly and the game is up.

Q: *This is exasperating and makes me feel angry, which I know does not help the cause.*

John: Relax and let go the focus on thought. See the truth of the statement 'What is wrong with right now if you're not thinking about it?' You are ever-free, ever-clear, whole and complete right here and right now.

## 24
# Knowing That You Are Cannot Be Doubted

*Question: I have a sense that thoughts can not be trusted, especially those that are self critical. But I am having a problem due to the doubt that I do not understand this. From your talk, it became clear to me that doubting is only more negative, self-critical thoughts. I see that.*

John: Yes. All of those are only appearances, images arising right in present clarity. This present clarity is what you are. Knowing that you are cannot be doubted. Actually, it is irrefutable, because you must be present and aware to have the doubt. That is the place to take your stand in order to rise completely above all possible doubts.

*Q: I have been experiencing a clarity that is very peaceful. I do not doubt awareness. However, I notice thought patterns that reoccur. They still generate feelings. I let them arise but do not hang onto them. I am starting a new job and sometimes feel concerns rising. I usually follow my breathing or feel my footsteps, and then I am fine again. I have been reading 'Awakening to the Natural State'. Your explanations are very clear. Do you have any suggestions on how to proceed from here?*

John: Continue to come back to present clarity and awareness. You are seeing that the thoughts are only conceptual patterns. To focus excessively on them creates more thoughts and feelings that reinforce the seeming problems. However, coming back to the sense of present awareness takes the belief or emotional attachment out of them. There is an immediate sense of clarity and freedom when you see this. Seeing this, there is naturally less inclination to follow conceptual thought, and you will effortlessly abide in present awareness. In fact, you are always only that natural state of pure presence-awareness, but following the habitual thoughts based on the imagined separate, defective self distracts us away from the ever-present simplicity of what is here. There is no need to fight thoughts. Gently return to the simple clear knowing that you are. Whether or not there are thoughts, you cannot ever separate from your true nature. Thoughts are only images arising and setting right in the clarity of presence-awareness.

# 25
# Communicating with Others

*Question: I read your first book about a year ago. But I must have not been ready to give up the search. Here I am again, and it is very clear and simple to me now. I feel like a huge weight has been lifted. There is a growing excitement that feels very deep, very ancient.*

John: This sounds right. That is exactly what this is. It is recognizing something in you that is very simple and clear and has been there all along. When you start to get a taste of this, it is incredibly exciting and alive. Your words show me that this is really striking home for you, not as concepts but something lived and sensed directly.

*Q: I am stuck on an issue with my grown children, who are struggling with some severe health issues. I cannot see how to interact with them. I feel peace in myself, but not when I talk to them. Can young people get this too, or is their own suffering their own path as it was for me?*

John: The best approach is to be clear and certain with your own understanding. This translates as your own sense of clarity and peace. This cannot be disturbed by people or circumstances. You ultimately come to see that the only thing that ever disturbs us is our own thoughts and imagination.

You may or may not talk about this openly, but if that clarity and peace is there, people will pick up on it. Whether or not they are interested will depend upon there own readiness and interest. If they are ready and interested, they will ask about it. If not, they will move along to wherever they are meant to be. One thing is certain, no one can prevent you from loving and caring for your children—not even they can! A very deep and profound type of love is what I would call self-less love. In this, the care, love and presence are shared in spite of what anyone else says or does or how they respond. If you love in this way and do not expect any particular response, your peace cannot be disturbed. As I see it, the universe has an intelligence and is guiding each one where he or she needs to be. Remain open to see what will unfold in each moment, without concern or prejudgment.

Whatever happens or not, you always remain poised in your real center. The presence-awareness that you are continues to shine through all circumstances and outcomes, regardless of what the mind thinks should be happening. If you align yourself with your true center instead of the thoughts and judgments in the mind, you cannot be moved or shaken from your center. Then all is fine as is, whatever happens. You see through to the deep essence supporting all appearances. If someone expresses an interest in these subjects, you can share your own understanding. If the interest is not there, you rest content knowing that everyone is always that clear presence of awareness and that they are unaffected by the appearance—whether they know it or not.

Q: *This is what I needed to hear. It is almost as if I needed permission to be peaceful even when my children are not. I see now how deeply this center can be 'held' and how powerful the clarity is when you say 'this cannot be disturbed by people or circumstances'. I see how I have let these things cover up or hide this presence-awareness in the past by going into my children's stories with them. It feels so wonderful to have the searching over!*

John: You have the basics of this. Everything you need is right there in that simple presence behind the thought 'I am'. That is the true nature that you cannot lose. From there, watch how life unfolds wonderfully and effortlessly.

# 26

# Awareness Is the Constant Background of Experiences

*Question: I continue to have moments of shining happiness, several seconds long. Today, while walking in the alley by a local bookstore, I felt a flash of amazing sweetness, as if life were a beautiful clear sea of happiness.*

John: As you settle in with the recognition of what is clear and present in you, you see that this is really the background or container in which all appearances arise. From the perspective of the mind and time, it appears as moments. But really, it is thoughts that arise sporadically and momentarily in and on this pure presence-awareness. You are catching the 'fragrance' of what this is. It is the recognition of a natural clarity and joy that was previously overlooked. It may appear as flashes of insight or joy as you notice it, but as you settle in with this, it is recognized as the natural, constant background of all appearances.

*Q: I continue to look into sensory awareness as a way to de-emphasize thought and notice presence.*

John: In noticing pure, immediate perception, the focus comes off of the exclusive involvement with conceptual thought. It is only in and through conceptual thought that problems and suffering are generated. When the focus is off of it the problems are no more.

*Q: I am trying to release my attachment to the memory of these moments and to cherish the present moment. Of course I cannot do much about my attachments except note them and whatever else is going on in the moment.*

John: The 'I' trying to release is another thought, another mental concept. It is best to simply see what is occurring and come back to notice and rest in the pure presence-awareness. Fighting or manipulating thought keeps you focused on it. To see without an agenda and rest as the undeniable awareness immediately takes the steam out of every concept.

# 27

# The Separate 'I' Is the Root Concept

*Question: Once this is truly seen and recognized, what do we do about all of the things going on in our life, for example, work, relationships, money and so on? Do they change at all?*

John: They might or might not. A key aspect of this approach is exposing wrong perceptions of ourselves that lead to suffering and separation. The root concept is the belief in the separate 'I', which is the basis of dualism and self-centered conceptual thinking. With that understood, the attachments and concerns about who and what we are, are resolved. Life is free to flow in whatever way it wants to. Experiences are no longer guided by false beliefs and attachments based on the belief in the self-center. Nor is there even any concept of there being a separate self or reference point of 'me' in the picture. Things may go on as before or may change, depending on the dictates of the situation and the innate intelligence that is running the show anyhow!

The concern and worry about what 'I' should do or not do fades out of the focus of interest. Life is a spontaneous arising in each moment. Thoughts, feelings, actions and decisions occur quite intelligently, but without reference to an imagined self-center. Anything can arise, but you remain rooted in the clear recognition of your true nature. Life becomes open, natural and joyous—not necessarily in an overt way. I am not talking about experiences here, but a subtle wordless knowing that everything is all right as is. And if things change, then that is all right, too.

*Q: When you talk to other people and they are sharing with you their problems about life, about their bad marriage or their work situation, do you personally offer advice regarding their specific situation? Or do you simply point them to their awareness and avoid giving direct advice or help in those areas?*

John: I have no blueprint at all. I have no idea what to say or why. I never talk about this subject with someone unless they express an interest. In general, I tend to point people back to the basic pointers, unless something specific comes up to say. I do not claim to be an authority in particular relative situations. My own experience is that when our identity is clear, everything takes care of itself.

See what your identity is. Then all the doubts and questions come into perspective. Ultimately, there is no 'you' or 'I' present to do or not do anything. See clearly what is true, and let everything flow naturally from that seeing. Even well-known 'sages' have said that they have no idea what they are going to do or say next, so we can probably relax about it also!

# 28

## You Are Not an Appearance in the Mind

*Q: You and others say you cannot reach 'it' through the mind.*

John: I will stand by this. This is about self-knowledge or knowing your true nature. What you are is not an appearance in the mind. So looking in the mind is not effective. That is like looking for a needle in a haystack when there is no needle in the haystack!

*Q: You have also stated that when you are interested in non-dual books that you are quite close to unfolding.*

John: You are neither close nor far away. Right here, right now, the natural state is shining in plain view. Discard the concepts of unfolding, awakening or 'getting it'. They are not needed. Come back to what is clear and present. Those concepts lead us away from the immediacy of what is pointed to.

*Q: So the mind is not the key to access or understand 'it'. That does make sense. But why do I have such deep resonance with what you are saying and yet continue to suffer, search and seek?*

John: You resonate with this because I am pointing to something clear and present in you that is already known at some deep, fundamental level. Suffering goes on as long as the belief in separation and the attendant self-centered concepts are taken as true.

*Q: There is a deep desperation here, just as you said you experienced after so much reading and listening to teachers.*

John: Bring the investigation back to the root. Clarify the fundamentals completely so there is no doubt left about who and what you are.

Q: *Do we really have any individual purpose, or is that also part of the drama of a so-called life?*

John: If you must have purpose, I would say that the purpose is to understand who you are and to discover a life free of suffering caused by an assumed separation from your true nature. But 'purpose' is really a concept created in thought in order to satisfy the mind. Life needs no purpose. It is. What appears is a spontaneous manifestation. Life, being, awareness and love do not have a purpose. They are. In the end, the answer is to resolve your identity. With the belief in separation removed, there is no need to live through mental concepts, including the concept of purpose.

Q: *You have stated that it is rare, if it does happen at all, for one to unfold through books.*

John: Books are words. Words live in memory. If you pursue the answer in words, you end up with mind stuff and overlook the root. There is no unfolding needed. Recognize what is present in you now. Drop the concept of unfolding and simply see the basics of what I am pointing to. Unfolding implies a future time and some special attainment. What I am pointing to has nothing to do with any of that. Your true nature is now. It is not a state, but an ever-present fact. This is pointed out. You can verify it for yourself.

Q: *What specific questions can I ask or what inquiry can I do, given the fact most non-dual books, such as yours, claim there is nothing I can do?*

John: I never say this. Many do, but it is an unclear view. See the basic pointers for yourself. Apply the pointers. See who and what you are and expose the roots of doubt and suffering. If there is nothing to do to end seeking and suffering, why talk about all this?

Q: *But the doing based on the separate 'I' is a distraction.*

John: Forget the doing or not doing. That is not the problem. As you are intuiting, the assumed 'I' sense is the central concept at the root of the mind's problems. That concept thrives because it is taken to be true, to be your identity. Who and what is this assumed entity? Can you find it? Is it real? Is this what you really are? This inquiry unwinds all the doubts and exposes your true state of present clarity. That is here now of course, but the fixation on conceptual thoughts turns us away from recognizing what is actually present. In the end, it is a matter of getting your doubts and questions resolved and simply abiding in and as the doubtless presence of awareness that you truly are.

## 29

# What Are We Looking For?

*Question: What are we all really looking for? What is the great human search for anyway?*

John: There are many ways to address this: to find what is true, to be at peace, to find love, to know God, to know yourself, to resolve suffering, to end doubt, to find harmony, to end separation. The list goes on. But these are all saying the same thing. All of these are fulfilled through knowing the truth of who you are. Enough questions! Probe into the one thing that can never doubted or questioned—the fact of your being. You undoubtedly are, as that sense of knowing presence. That is with you now. Without this there can be no experiences, questions or anything else for that matter. What is that knowing presence, that true nature that is with you right now? The answer cannot be found in the mind through thoughts or concepts. It is direct, immediate, non-conceptual knowledge.

## No 'Me' Left at All

*Question:* The cloudiness went away when I stopped giving it power. In the past, I remember feeling that there was this sense of 'me' I had to worry about. I had to plan for it and understand it. It stretched out for miles in either direction, and it was overwhelming. Then that 'me' started to include less and less as chunks of the past and future started falling away leaving me with less and less 'me'. Finally there was nothing left but right now, and there was no 'me' left at all.

John: Everything you need is present for you. There is nothing more to understand. Every attempt to do so brings you back to the mind and away from the immediate clarity that is already present.

# 31
# The Mind Creates All Doubts and Problems

*Question: I think perhaps that we use the word 'spontaneous' in slightly different senses. I simply mean 'unpremeditated', but I think that you mean that thoughts just 'happen by themselves'. I can see, now, that your usage must be correct. If there is no 'me', who can there be to premeditate or, indeed, think? I agree that I cannot predict my next thought. Although my thoughts and communications are shaped and directed by previous thoughts, my conditioning and my personality, they must actually arise spontaneously. Incredible, but true! The thought now arises that a period is needed to let the pointers, this new way of looking at things, sink in.*

John: Before the next thought, feeling, emotion or state arises, you are undeniably present and aware as the one to whom all those appear. That knowing presence that you are does not come and go. All the conditioned thoughts will have you looking elsewhere for some answer that you do not have. But it is the mind that creates all the doubts, questions and problems. Your true nature is not subject to doubts. To abide as that is the key point. This is the natural state that is shining in plain view. It is right here, right now. It is seeing your true nature as present awareness. Just this, and nothing else.

# The Obviousness of 'What Is'

*Question: Just over a week ago I leaped out of bed in the middle of the night with the absolute self-evident awareness that there was no time, that all memories of the past and anticipation of the future are quite simply thoughts arising right now. I had previously understood this conceptually, but here it was slapping me in the face with the obviousness of it. This remained with me. At the same time there was a sense of a huge implication for something which, paradoxically, took a couple of days before it too started slapping me in the face—if the past and future are presently-arising thoughts, then what am 'I'?*

*Somewhere between those two events, I listened to your song. It was during a period of immense, gentle, effortless silence on a peaceful Sunday afternoon while watching the clouds go by. Everything seemed so appropriate. What followed was a week of life living itself absolutely effortlessly. There were no worries about time, just being present, even while being late for work, squabbling with my family, watching the clouds or enduring a hangover. Things were also falling away, such that I was not so much discovering things as noticing what was always there and, equally, realizing what was not there. I recall looking down at my feet resting on the floor and seeing the mind call them 'my feet' and that what they were resting on was the 'not-me' floor. It was absolutely clear that this was an entirely arbitrary distinction. I tried to write this down at the time, but there is no meaningful way to describe the utter simplistic obviousness of 'what is' and of the operation of the conceptualizing or dualizing thought occurring within 'this'.*

John: This is all well said, and I cannot add anything. This is the way things are. At some point, it is simply seen. Once you see this, you can never go back to the old view with any force or sustained belief. However, the old mental views, out of habit, may arise. These are the residual doubts, beliefs and assumptions based on duality and belief in separation. If we put these lenses back on by believing and focusing on the thoughts and taking them to be real, we overlook the clear seeing of what is. Once you get a sense of the clear perspective and realize that the duality is driven by old, unexamined concepts picked up in years of not knowing any better, a natural intelligence arises that pulls the energy of belief out of the conceptual mechanism.

Q: *Yes. Unfortunately, the 'I' appears to have returned this week, as if a large and persistent cloud squatting on the horizon. I am currently feeling something of a sense of loss for, ironically, 'nothing'. The old pattern of trying to attain or grasp that which has been seen to be unattainable and ungraspable by 'me' has re-established itself! What occurred is now something in memory. The treadmill of trying to regain 'it' has heaved into motion with all its inherent friction and utter pointlessness.*

John: The best approach at this juncture is to clearly understand what is happening. I was cycling through this kind of thing for years. However, things cleared up quickly when I at last understood the mechanism, so to speak, of what was occurring. Presence, awareness, or whatever you want to call it, has not gone anywhere. You are the same now as last week. Nothing has changed. The experience of separation, individuality or 'me' and the attendant flow of self-centered ideas and experiences is a chain of conceptual thought based on an assumption of separation. Apart from those thoughts, there is really nothing going on! You have not changed. The nature of what is has not changed. All is as it was and has always been. The erroneous thoughts are taken as true and some focus goes into them. That is all.

At some point with this, there is a recognition that the 'me' and me-related thoughts are simply creations in the mind. Being clearly aware that the whole affair is a production in thought undercuts the beliefs. Ultimately, the seeing dawns that all the thoughts are based on the belief in a separate person. On investigation the separate person is found to be absent. In other words, the whole superstructure is based on an assumed person that was never there! Yet presence is, awareness is, your true nature is—and this is undeniable. These kinds of things are pointed out in various ways and that natural intelligence in you resonates. You then have a look and see it for yourself. There are many ways to phrase all this. It gets down to seeing what is true about yourself along with, as needed, questioning the false beliefs about ourselves that we have taken as true.

*Q: I am planning to attend the talks of a certain teacher. It is a four or five hour drive from here, but reading about your own much longer journey 'down under', I sense that any apparent obstacles to the journey are trivial in the extreme. This is especially clear when I realize that I once again may see that any further journeys are needless.*

John: Remember, we are not talking about an event in the future. You are present and aware now. All the concepts and beliefs based on apparent dualism are arising right here and now in present awareness. In no way are you ever separate or apart from presence, even if the mind says otherwise. It is simply not true. This is not about going anywhere or getting anything that is not already clearly present.

## 33
## Self-Centered Stories

*Question: I had a great experience on Saturday morning. Wrestling with several emotional issues, I decided to be with the feelings in my body. I happened to have a stomachache. All of a sudden, the emotional-mental component vanished. I no longer had those issues. My stomach immediately felt better. All I did was tune in to the body with the intention of feeling my emotions.*

John: Tuning into immediate sensations of the world or the body is a useful way to take the exclusive focus out of conceptual thought. This is another clue that getting focused in the mind leads us to overlook problem-free, natural presence-awareness. Notice that whether you are wrapped up in the mind or not, you still exist and are clearly present and aware. Your natural identity is not related to the contents of the mind. We get involved in thought because we take it to either describe or contain our true nature. But it does neither.

As this sinks in, the interest in the self-centered stories in the mind wanes considerably, and the natural openness of presence-awareness shines. Your true nature is natural, effortless presence, which has no problems. It is innately free of psychological suffering. It is not an emotional state. It is not something to wait for in the future. It is the ever-present basis on which all sensations, thoughts and feelings appear. How can there be anything at all without the presence of awareness? This is shining at all times and cannot be doubted.

# 34
## Emptiness and Nothingness

*Question: You and others have written that the only thing we can know for certain is that we exist. Yes, that makes sense! But I get confused when I try to understand that the ego is a fiction. That seems to suggest we do not exist, much less know anything for certain.*

John: We both exist and do not exist. We exist as that undeniable and very clear presence of awareness. However, the image or mind-created entity, which we have taken to be who we are, is not who we actually are. In fact, there is nothing observable that is our essential nature. We undoubtedly are something, but in terms of the appearance, or objectively, we are not findable as any particular thing. That is where the notion of emptiness or 'nothingness' comes in. Your true nature is present and cognizant but utterly clear and empty by nature. From another angle, everything that appears is not separate from awareness, so you could say that the essence of everything is your essence also. This naturally might lead you to say 'I am everything that appears', which is also true. But the separate entity that we may have taken ourselves to be is not findable. It is only a notion. It has only an assumed existence. If we think it is present, did we ever actually find it?

*Q: My second question is about suffering. There is the intensity of life's apparent suffering, the ravages of cancer, the bloody carnage of a fierce battle, sexual and physical abuse and so on.*

John: What you are describing is pain, which is very different from psychological suffering based on the belief in a limited entity. Be clear on this point.

*Q: Do those things create the sense of going 'back and forth' between awareness and the illusory me?*

John: No. The appearances are not the determining factor in the experience of suffering. Suffering is only an appearance in the mind. The only thing that ever causes suffering is our own imagination, not bare events.

*Q: But if you have just had a minor argument with a friend, it seems like it would be a lot easier to return to being conscious of awareness than if you are going through massive physical pain. Does the pain pull you into the ego's realm, or, just the opposite, does it act as a beloved reminder? Maybe it depends on one's level of understanding?*

John: There is a confusion here. There is no returning to awareness and no one to return to it. You are ever and always pure knowing itself. This is the sword that cuts the Gordian knot of conceptual confusion and doubt. Everything that appears, appears on the support of presence-awareness. You are that presence-awareness. The ego is imaginary. All the subsequent concepts are imagined. There is no real 'ego's realm'. The mind is imagining separation and bondage where there is none actually present.

# 35

# What You Are and What You Are Not

*Question: I find it difficult to get beyond the concept that there is no separate person. Naturally, I do not walk around saying the words 'I am a separate person' all the time.*

John: Yes, and when you are not saying these words, you do not fall apart. You do not lose your being. So those words are not what you are.

*Q: But the body that is with me everywhere, the separate thoughts that relate to that body and the circumstances surrounding it make it seem that there is a separateness that defines me.*

John: First, the body aspect. In direct evidence the body is, like everything, an appearance in awareness. The classic identification is that 'I am the body'. But this is a learned concept.

*Q: If I look for the character Jane, I do not locate one.*

John: Precisely.

*Q: However, I do find a collection of thoughts and sensations that seem unique to what I have called Jane for all these years. Is this not a person?*

John: The seeming person is a collection of memories and ideas, but other than those, there is nothing substantial or enduring at all. It is like the wrappings of a mummy. But in this case, you strip away the bandages and there is nothing present at the center. All the thoughts and identities are memories about someone. But other than the ideas, there is really no one present, except as an assumption. So, to your point, the apparent person is a collection of memories. But there is no substantial entity or thing to whom they refer. It is a self-referencing mechanism without any self. Seeing that is enough to dismantle the whole conceptual façade. You are not really contradicting what I am saying but rather confirming it!

More importantly, even granting the existence of thoughts and memories in the mind, are you a collection of ideas and memories? Ideas, images and memories appear and disappear, but you are none of those things. None of those are your abiding essence. They are appearances to you. You are aware of those things. Sometimes they are present in awareness, sometimes not. But there is an undeniable sense of being or presence that is entirely unrelated to specific ideas, identifications and memories.

*Q: I can understand how this might be a habitual response that I fall into because of years of misguided thinking, but it still feels real.*

John: A mirage looks real. But it is an appearance. There is no denying the appearance and the assumption that is real. But you can investigate it to see if it is, in fact, real. Of course, we assume we are separate persons. Of course, we assume that this perception is real. Of course, we live under the belief that we are a limited, separate being apart from the source. But this is precisely what is pointed out as an illusion. A careful examination shows that all psychological doubt and suffering is rooted in the assumed limited, defective self. This is the core insight of many great spiritual traditions. Each of us, in our own way, is called upon to verify whether these findings are true or not. I would suggest that if this belief continues unquestioned, suffering is the inevitable result.

*Q: Trying to understand the absence of a 'me' feels like a movement of the mind, rather than a true understanding.*

John: Good. This should not be a mental operation at all, so it is good to see that. Otherwise, this all becomes dry words. That is why the seeing of your true nature is a key part of this. Is your present awareness a theory or a fact? This cannot be known in the mind. It is completely non-conceptual and immediate understanding.

*Q: There is also a feeling that I must do some sort of practice to let this sink in. After all, there have been thirty-five years of seeking and clinging on tenaciously to my identity!*

John: Who is to do a practice? Practice is done by an assumed someone trying to get somewhere. Once you launch off on that, the very ideas you are trying to question are assumed to be real. Without a belief in an 'I' that is separate and incomplete, there is no need for any practice. That is why practices tend to reinforce the very thing they are trying to expose. Practice does not get at the roots of the issue. It does not address the fundamental cause. That is why after years, we still cycle in this stuff. The root of the problem is a conceptual error, a wrong belief, in other words, ignorance. Ignorance is not eradicated through practice, but through knowledge. At best, practices are a palliative that may suppress the symptoms of ignorance but will definitely not yield a cure. That is why people taking that route are often still suffering decades later.

*Q: Sometimes I just sit and allow things to arise. But I find that the thoughts take over, even if it is trying to control the thoughts through meditation or concentration techniques.*

John: Exactly. The proof is in the pudding. The roots of the whole mechanism are still active and driving the conceptual framework, along with the residual belief in it.

*Q: Sometimes I ponder the pointers. If I am gentle, this can feel okay. But doing nothing goes strongly against the grain of my intense desire to be free.*

John: I do not believe in 'doing nothing'. This is not the message of non-duality. Some people think so, but this is a mistaken view. I advocate clear seeing. The non-dual pointers demand a very clear and penetrating investigation of things. It is not intellectual philosophy at all. It is a first-hand verification, based on one's own direct experience, to see what is true and undeniable about ourselves. In conjunction with this is the exposing of false concepts, which we have believed without proof. This often occurs in the context of living dialogue. Book reading is rarely sufficient. Email is a pale attempt to do this. Talking on the phone or in person is better for most of us. For most of us, there is a strong habit to follow this stuff in the mind. But experience shows the results are marginal. The mind has very little value in all this. It is the wrong tool.

You know that you are. Thoughts, feelings and sensations come and go. You remain. This is a fact. It is not a theory. The essential pointing is directly to that undeniable presence of awareness that you are. Make that the focus of your consideration and all the other pointers make much more sense. If you overlook that, it all becomes mental speculation and dry theory. Your existence is not a theory. Verify these points to your full satisfaction. Do not take any of them on blind faith.

## 36
## Recognizing Things in Awareness

*Question: I read a few pages of your book every day to get the pointers on a consistent basis. I noticed that in all the books on non duality, few of them mention anything about vision. Last October I experienced a day where I saw nature in such clearness and purity. It came and went, but now it is very consistent in my everyday life. I do not notice the clear vision much until I go outside and look at the trees. Then I can see and feel their aliveness jump right out, as if another dimension has been added. At other times I get carried away by thought and dullness takes over. Has anybody ever mentioned something like this to you? I figure this is one of the byproducts of non-separation. Perhaps it is activated by a raise in vibrational frequency?*

John: When the focus drops out of exclusive identification with conceptual thought there is more space available to recognize other things going on in awareness. This includes sensing, noticing the body, noticing people and things and so on. Often, what is being perceived by the senses seems more clear and vivid. Awareness is incredibly alive, bright, clear and intense by nature. It radiates its living light on everything that appears within it. This becomes apparent when there is less fixation on thinking.

# Flip-Flopping

*Question: I still seem to be flip-flopping with all of this. The ups are very up and the downs are very down. I feel very constricted and frustrated. But it occurred to me today that the basis of the problem is the feeling of being in something called a body that is in a universe. This sense of containment is the cause of the feeling of being limited and bound by time and space and a victim to events. For most of my life this feeling of being inside a body in a universe has perplexed and frustrated me. Today it became very clear. Life is not the problem! But feeling as if I am inside life creates loads of problems and frustrations. I have never been able to get my head around the 'fact' of being in here! Assuming that I am in here has led to all kinds of effort at developing, improving, progressing and so on.*

*Today it was clear that this conflict-filled life will never end as long as I believe I am in something such as a body or a universe. In other words, it seems that everything is fine just as long as I am not inside of anything. Without that there is a lot of space and acceptance. Does this make any sense? I hope so! I guess whatever the thoughts may be, if they provide a feeling of peace they cannot be bad!*

John: As many people have pointed out over the ages, the thought 'I am this body' is one of the main concepts at the root of suffering. This could also be phrased as 'I am in the body'. This notion is uncomfortable and awkward because it is not true. Awareness, your real nature, is not encased or cooped up in a body. Go by immediate experience and see that the body and all else arise as appearances within your nature of awareness. This brings things into clear view right away, and the tension and conflict dissolve. The presence of the body as such is not an issue. If you are not conceptualizing about it, all is clear, peaceful and fine as is, body or no body. As usual, it is the concept in the mind and the subsequent belief in it that is the source of the conflict. Even the concept appearing in mind is powerless. It is a mere thought passing through awareness. Awareness does not change its nature. You are that awareness. It is only the belief in the thought that is troublesome. The thought is believed because it is assumed as true. However, questioning that concept exposes its falseness. Then you no longer believe it. The freedom is right there, immediately in that seeing.

# 38

## Pause Thought and Simply Be

*Question: It occurred to me that knowing more or accumulating more is going in the wrong direction. I reflected back to what you have often said—that we really do not know much at all beyond our natural state. Seeing the futility of trying to know things and then giving up the knowing stops this sense of awkwardness and conflict, right? I mean, our natural state of aliveness is not going anywhere. What is coming and going are the ups and downs, the 'now I get it' and 'now I don't'. When things seem to make sense and feel nice this is not any different from when things feel all wrong. Both states are made of beliefs, either fitting together nicely or jarring with each other. It is, as you say, all in the believing. Believing leads to holding onto things and trying to maintain a fixed understanding. I guess it is just seeing that believing in any statement is unnecessary, because we already have what we need—our constant natural state.*

John: Yes. It is not about getting or not getting anything. What is, is undeniable present awareness. Everything appears within that. It is all an expression within that. You are what you are. All ideas about what we are, are only more ideas. To attempt to pin anything down in the mind is futile. Your natural being is not contained or even known by the mind. Basically, the answer is not in the mind. Seeing this, you stop looking for an answer where it will not be found. You are present and aware. Pause thought and simply be. Notice that there is nothing wrong. There are no problems or suffering unless you are thinking about them. So the mind is creating all problems. They are all imaginary. Seeing this, you stop chasing thoughts and concepts in the mind. You relax, knowing that you cannot be anything but that presence-awareness.

That is incredibly clear, vivid, alive and open. What you are looking for is contained right in this immediate awareness that you are. Everything appears and disappears in present awareness. It has no independent existence apart from this. So it must be, in the end, only that. That is non-duality. What is wrong if you are not conceiving it to be wrong? All is that. You are that. Everything else is an unfounded concept that falls to pieces when you look at it.

# There Is No Realization

*Question: Through reading various books I reached the conclusion that observation without evaluation is key for realization.*

John: First of all, there is no realization. Because there is no realization, no technique or process is needed. There is only a confusion because we do not see clearly what we are. This means that we are already what we are. Nothing new is brought in. The key is not some new attainment, but simply clarifying what our real nature is. The mistaken identity is what is driving all the doubts and confusion. From the position of imagined separation, the mind generates a lot of dualistic, self-referencing concepts. Then we view the world through those dualistic concepts, judgments and evaluations. But these are the effects of the deeper cause. My suggestion is to tackle the issue at the core.

There are many ways to talk about this. Pure seeing or knowing is prior to the conceptual filters. Coming back to pure, non-conceptual seeing or knowing reveals life outside of the conceptual boxes. Experiencing life beyond belief in self-centered, dualistic thinking is natural and effortless freedom. The truth is that your nature of presence-awareness is already outside of concepts. In recognizing that, you stand free of the assumed conceptual bondage.

*Q: Until I read your books, I believed that I should recondition my thoughts to be 'non-evaluative'. Now I am seeing that I may have had the right idea but the wrong perspective.*

John: Reconditioning the mind is much too involved in the appearance. Nothing needs to change. Just see what is going on. That seeing is enough to dismantle any residual belief in the separate self and the concepts built on that notion.

Q: *Perhaps observation without evaluation means observing the conditioned thoughts that arise without becoming attached to those thoughts?*

John: The thoughts are not really where the problem lies. Why pay so much attention to mere passing thoughts? This is about self-knowledge, not studying the mind. Remember, the answer is not in the mind. Who or what is aware of the mind? That is the essence. There is an undeniable presence that is both existent and aware, that is cognizing the mind and all else. That is what you are. That has nothing to do with mind, body or world. All those come and go, but you, as that presence-awareness, remain. This is not about changing the mind. Simply see that the mind is an appearance, a shadow subsisting on a deeper presence. Not noting this, we are looking for answers in the content of the mind. Let the mind be. It is fine for dealing with appearances. You are not an appearance, and so the mind is not the right tool for self-knowledge.

Q: *For those who have not realized their true nature as the substratum of thoughts, feeling and memories—wouldn't it be better to live with others who, though perhaps not fully realized, had at least pacified their egos to a degree through reconditioning thought?*

John: Do not build this up into some grand concept of people who have 'it'! There is only one true nature and it is shining right within you. You are that. It does not reside 'out there', much less are there special beings who have it, which always implies that we do not! Recognize and abide as the true nature that you are. Get to know yourself. Live with yourself. Do not follow thoughts and concepts in the mind about a person, the seeming 'you', and attend to that while overlooking your true nature. All anyone could possibly do by way of help is to point you back to the fact that the one thing to know is your own present awareness.

*Q: Gandhi did not seem to me to have been enlightened, but through strong convictions and will power he was able to act 'as if'.*

John: Gandhi, like everyone and everything, is only that presence-awareness, so why the need to act 'as if'? It is only one who imagines himself to be separate who needs to act 'as if'. But tell me, are you really a separate person apart from presence-awareness? This is what needs to be verified. All the problems come from this assumption.

*Q: Please forgive me if these questions sound strange to you!*

John: All questions are based on the assumption that we exist as separate, limited beings apart from reality. That notion is what is strange! All actions, questions, assertions and so on tend to miss the essence until this core assumption is examined to see if it is even true.

# 40

## Love, Joy, Peace and Happiness

*Question: I have been interested in an energetic transmission called 'deeksha'. I have to admit that I am enjoying it. I try to look at it as an interesting experience with no one claiming it. I experience it like I do other emotions. It is just energy without a story of enlightenment or awakening. It is an enjoyable experience!*

John: Enjoy whatever comes up. There can be no deeksha apart from presence-awareness. It is yet another passing experience. As it comes, it goes. You remain. Love, joy, peace and happiness are other terms for being and awareness. They are not separate experiences. If happiness is imagined to be something apart from us, then we will naturally be drawn to those sources we imagine providing happiness. Clear seeing comes in and exposes this as well. Then you see that happiness and joy never come from experiences, but are an emanation of your true nature.

Happiness and joy are the feeling, so to speak, of presence-awareness. From the position of the mind, your true nature looks like awareness. From the position of changing appearances, it is the sense of presence or existence. From the position of the heart or feeling, it is love. All happiness, joy and love reside in you. Metaphorically, this is termed your 'heart'. Happiness is only ever felt within you, not outside. There is really no joy or happiness in experiences, objects or events. That is a total impossibility because happiness is not an object. It is only ever felt within. There is only one thing that is within, and that is your true nature. This is existence, awareness and happiness or peace. Happiness is not talked about much because it comes in automatically with the recognition of you true nature of awareness. Just as awareness is free and unbounded, so is love or happiness. It is a profound peace, joy and happiness. That is why deeksha may lose its charm ultimately. The joy promised cannot really compare to what is recognized in the clear, immediate recognition of presence-awareness. The joy obtained from those things is not even coming from those things, but is only a reflection from the actual source within ourselves.

# 41
## Your Awareness Is Not in a Book

*Question: I bought your second book and was very surprised to read in it that you feel reading books will not result in awakening. You might have written this at the beginning of your first book. Then I would have known not to bother buying it! This approach is hardly helpful. I have only recently come across these pointers to awareness, having reached the age of seventy-three and being a Methodist preacher. I thought that at last I had found the answer. Now I am not so sure.*

John: The point is that your true nature is not contained in any book. The books appear in your awareness. It is not saying that understanding is not available, because it is most definitely so. But, as you cannot drink water from the map of a lake, neither can you recognize your true nature by reading about it in a book. The words are pointers. Follow the pointers and recognize that what you are seeking is your own nature. That is clear and present as the undeniable sense of being and awareness that enables you to say 'I know I am'. The words 'I know I am' are not you. You are present as that which is knowing the words and all else.

The point made in the book is that the answer is your own being. Recognize that and all the answers are right there for you. The purpose of my statements was to put the book into proper perspective so you would observe or discover what the book is pointing to. That is all. Of course reading books will not result in knowing your true nature any more than reading a menu will fill your belly with real food. The best pointer, in my view, is through living contact. In absence of that, a book can be a resource. It can tell you where to look, but you must do the looking.

## [Follow up]

*Q: Thank you very much. Things are much clearer now!*

John: I am glad to hear that that particular doubt is behind you! Let my book and any other you might read simply be a reminder of that clear and solid presence of awareness within you. Make that your anchor and your foundation. Come back to a clear recognition of who and what you are. What you are is the undeniable sense of knowing presence that is aware of all thoughts, objects and experiences. That is not a body, mind or object. It is the inner light or spirit in you. The body constantly changes, but your being remains clear and bright and has not changed throughout life. The body appears and disappears in the light of your true nature. The universe arises and sets in that awareness that you are. The awareness in you is the light of the world, because it is only in the light of presence-awareness that the world arises. Saints and sages throughout history have found their true nature to be that one light. You, too, are that light. You are not separate or different from those beings, because the divine is one and shines alike in everyone as their own true self.

## 42

## Life Flows Effortlessly

*Question: I feel more at ease now with the pointers. We live in an intelligent universe that responds fluidly in laying out our life. Only the imaginary separate self hinders that by focusing on resistant thoughts. Once the phantom self is seen for what it is, then life flows effortlessly. Seeing this, it is good to be alive!*

John: You have a good, solid resonance with the basics of this. Trust in your own seeing of what you know to be true. The recognition of presence-awareness is clear for you. Let that be your touchstone. That is the undeniable and constant presence of your true nature. Before the mind arises, you already are. The closest the mind can come to this is the thought 'I am'. Yet that thought is not what you are, because you are there whether or not that thought is present. All thoughts, feelings and objects appear in this that you are. Without presence-awareness, nothing is. Presence-awareness is naturally and effortlessly present as the pure sense of knowing that shines constantly behind the thought 'I am'. Everything else the mind says about you is an erroneous concept, a false belief. See thoughts as mere thoughts and there can be no suffering or bondage. Awareness is ever-present and ever free.

## 43
## The Game Is Up

*Question: There is now a frequent, spontaneous movement from appearances back to awareness, to 'no thing'. There is an arising of joy in that. It is uncaused joy, the joy of being, of recognizing my true nature. Maybe it has something to do with the deeksha (energetic transmission) I have received from a group I am involved with. Perhaps it is happening on it is own and I give deeksha the credit. There are other experiences, too. They are nothing particularly amazing. I do not associate them with my true nature. I keep remembering all the experiences Nisargadatta Maharaj said he had, but he kept ignoring them and returning to the source of those appearances. I try very hard not to lose sight of this.*

*I was corresponding with a teacher who pointed out that awakening was not what I wanted it to be. At first I thought it was, and then there was a strange dissociation with no joy. She experienced that as well. That is when you have seen the emptiness but not the fullness yet. She believes that there is awakening and then in six months you finally see it. That is what happened with her and some others. They all got a little crazy in between, and the renewed suffering brought them back. The woman I am corresponding with seems to have the same belief—that the final seeing comes after the suffering reappears. I do not think there are any rules to this. You tend to teach whatever your experience was. That is not to say I will not go back into suffering, but it is not a driving force at the moment. I guess there is nothing left to do but stay focused on the source of all this and watch it play itself out. What a crazy ride!*

John: All of the talk of awakening, how it works, how it works for some and so forth is more mind stuff to be seen through and dropped. It keeps the conceptual mind on the boil looking for one more event, one more confirmation, one more reason to stay engaged in the drama! This is not a matter of beliefs and peoples' experiences and how it worked for them, however great or famous they may appear to the mind. At some point with all this, it will hit you between the eyes—the game is up. There are no more reasons, no more 'what ifs', no more dependencies, no more future time, no more comparison with others, no more projections of happiness on situations or circumstances. You are ever and always that presence-awareness. Here and now it is totally full to the brim with all the peace and uncaused joy you can ever want. Seeking joy in circumstances and events is innocent enough, but it is due to confusion—like seeing the moonlight and thinking the light comes from the moon. That basic error keeps us on the move, chasing experiences, emotional states, relationships that promise love and all the rest. At some point we see that all the life, joy, light and love is coming from the true nature itself.

A few of the false concepts that keep us stringing along are the belief in a special awakening and the idea of getting some happiness that we imagine is not present. Then there is the belief that special ones 'out there' have 'it'. If you look deeply into all these ideas, you will see they are all flawed. However, they keep the mind on the hunt looking for something new and different and thinking we are not there. The truth is that 'you', under those conditions, will never, ever get 'there'. However, you will at some point question those beliefs and they will lose their grip. Then you will realize that you, as a separate one, are not even there, and that there is nowhere to go and nothing to get.

You have already seen everything there is to see. However, there is some doubt or lack of confidence in that seeing, so there is an inclination to take a spin back into the mind in case there might be something there! As long as the notion is present that happiness derives from an experience, the mind is caught in a duality. Our concept has been to separate happiness or joy from what we are. Who would be interested in knowing their true nature if there were no joy in it! Of course one goes off searching for experiences in that case.

The idea that one recognizes one's true nature but there is no happiness in that recognition needs to come under some inspection. We are so habituated to associating happiness with experiences that we overlook it outside of that context. This demands some deeper inquiry and consideration. Most people associate happiness with experiences and, of course, run after experiences in hopes of attaining happiness. Like I said, that is like searching for light on the moon. There is no light on the moon. The light is only a reflection of the source. Until this is realized, the clear and steady recognition of our true nature is not possible because we cannot sit still long enough, so to speak, to recognize it. The mind will produce another tantalizing thought and we are off to the races chasing the next book, teacher, fad or whatever it is.

You have the means within yourself to see through this game of the mind and understand that what you are seeking is what you already are. Then the seeking ends and you remain as you are. There is a clear knowing of that. It is not a grand realization or awakening, just knowing and being what you are here and now. The point is this. Cease to follow the thoughts and beliefs in the mind and—here and now—you abide as that one true nature. It is full with clarity and happiness beyond measure. No experience in the world compares to the direct seeing and knowing of your true nature. It is like the difference between a painted sun and the actual sun. You are the sun of suns, pure presence-awareness itself.

## The End of the Story

*Question: Another series of 'looking elsewhere and into the future for what I am' seizures have ended. That kind of activity can go on forever, as you well know. I am fed up with that game. If that conversation starts up in consciousness again, it is more endless promises that will never pan out. What I am looking for is here now. What is this 'I' that is looking but another movement in consciousness? I was reporting this to a friend last night and she said it is a process for her. I saw that that word 'process' is very tricky. It seems like a process in time, but the mind can latch onto that and run for months, years, lifetimes so that the sense of separation has an excuse to continue. What is this 'process' happening in? This light of awareness. Then the mind can get embarrassed about what a fool it has been. That is a good one. It is only more fuel for continuing the search. Whatever is done, or not done, is done in this presence. That is the end of the story. The focus can return to what is already and always here. In realizing that, whatever arises is seen from that ground of awareness, not from what is changing or deepening. What is deepening is deepening in what we are. And what we are has no future.*

John: You are sharing some very clear insights here. I was chasing the future and waiting for experiences for years, until it got pointed out to me that time is a mental concept and no experience lasts. To put it in other terms, there is no 'enlightenment' in the future. This is one of those 'full stop' propositions that drops the mind dead in its tracks. Even enlightenment itself is a concept because you are walking around in full, present, alive presence-awareness all day long. In no way can you seriously maintain you are separate from this. That is the essence of it.

Then what happens? The whole house of cards simply collapses. The bottom falls out because every concept in the mind is only an idea arising in present awareness. They are all based on the idea that you are not yet there. Who? Where? Exposing that false idea immediately invalidates every other concept built upon it. You remain marvelously present, aware, alive—and it is so effortless and natural. When the focus goes out of the mind stuff, the ever-present clarity and joy of life are there, like the sun peaking out from behind the parting clouds. That clarity stays with you because it is your real nature. You cannot get out of who and what you are, even if you try. You cannot move away from what you are. How can you? At most, the mind can say 'I am not there'. But what is that except another thought based on imagined separation? See it as a thought and the ever-present presence is right there as plain as day.

## 45

## Awareness and Seeing

*Question: This is a picayune mind question, but it seems to persist. As I walk about during the day, there is a sporadic sense that awareness is all there is, that there is this all-encompassing seeing going on.*

John: Keep it direct and simple. All throughout the day, awareness is. All sensing, thinking, feeling, knowing and acting requires the presence of awareness. It is not a mystic state, but a necessary fact. Can you have any thought, perception or feeling without it being registered in awareness? That is what this is pointing to. No shifts or insights are needed.

*Q: From time to time, thoughts come in.*

John: In the awareness itself, correct?

*Q: If I am gentle with the thoughts and do not take them seriously, they usually fade in intensity.*

John: In actual experience, thoughts only last for a split second and disappear. That is why it is sometimes said that thoughts are self-liberating. There is no need to do anything with them because they do not last long enough for you to be able do anything with them.

*Q: I think, however, that I have made the mistake of turning the concept of seeing into something linked to visual phenomena. Perhaps I have read passages depicting something taking it all in, seeing everything even when the thoughts come in. When I close* my eyes, it seems impossible to have the same sense of awareness, particularly of seeing. Intellectually, I grasp the idea that if awareness is all there is, then seeing is still going on. But the concept does not resonate. The mind cannot take it in. I imagine you responding 'relax, the mind cannot and never will understand'!

John: Do not link awareness only to seeing. That is too limiting. All the senses, feelings and thoughts are registered or known due to the fact that you are present and aware. Do not consider awareness to be some special state of seeing. It is the everyday, ordinary sense of awareness. That knowing presence is registering your thoughts, feelings and sensations right now. That knowing presence is what you are.

Q: I was hung up on the words 'awareness' and 'seeing'. Do you think substituting the word 'all-ness' for 'awareness' or asking myself 'who is this that is trying so hard to figure it all out?' would be a better way to approach it?

John: You are overcomplicating things. As I said, it is not a special seeing at all. It is simply the fact of present awareness. You are present and aware, aren't you? That is what is being pointed to. We imagine it must be some complicated experience or special seeing. Let that concept go and realize that you are naturally and effortlessly that which is present and aware. Thinking and searching leads back into the mind and away from the simplicity of it.

# 46

# Without You, the Universe Is Not

*Question: I have been doing a lot of looking. It has all been good. It arises spontaneously, too. But I was associating it with having recently received a deeksha initiation, rather than my own looking. I can see the discrepancy. I recently read something interesting in a spiritual book. It said, if anything you are doing gives you hope then you are going down the mental rabbit trail, basically. I am quite aware that 'hope' has been a factor in my experiences lately, no matter what my rationalizations were. I cannot really deny that.*

John: Notice one simple thing. All that appears depends on your own presence. Without awareness what can be? Energetic experiences or anything else have relevance only because you are there to perceive them. You may give those things all the worth, but without you the universe cannot even appear! So do not imagine you are separate and in need of something. The universe needs you in order to appear. If this sounds far fetched, consider what the universe would look like if there were no awareness! You are that awareness. We often sell ourselves short and then suffer the pains of separation and limitation. Basically, you are not a poor, limited seeker in need of a fix. Present awareness is the only abiding reality, and you are that.

## 47
# Are You Free of the False Sense of Self?

*Question: Are you completely free from the identification with the 'I' entity? By 'I', I mean the false sense of self.*

John: This question is based on a misunderstanding. It is in reference to a seeming 'I'. A seeming 'I' cannot free itself from the notion of a seeming 'I'. It is circular and irresolvable at that level. One is left trying to free a seeming self of a seeming 'false' self. However, there can be a seeing that there is no 'I' present, except as a concept. What we are is clearly not a thought. One cannot meaningfully say 'I am free of the "I"' because that is still in reference to an 'I'!

*Q: It is my understanding that the 'I' thought is what obscures the present moment awareness or takes us out of present moment awareness like the clouds blocking the sun.*

John: Present awareness is never obscured. You are present and aware right now, correct? Is that obscured? You can never leave or move away from your true nature. That is why when you begin to approach this based on seeing the positive knowledge of what you are, rather than trying to negate obstacles, it is usually more direct.

*Q: Still, I am curious, how does one negate the 'I'?*

John: The notion of the separate 'I' is only the assumption that we exist as something separate and apart from presence-awareness. The 'I' is not an entity with any substance. It is a wrong assumption. With this assumption present we begin to look for this 'I' in the appearance and mistake ourselves to be something we are not, for example, the body, senses or mind. The so-called false 'I' is not an actual entity to be negated. It is an assumption that is exposed as false by seeing the true position. Everything that appears is only a passing appearance. None of those things can possibly be the essence of what you are. They are not 'I'.

What thing is the 'I'? No thing! There is no thing that is 'I'. The idea that something in the appearance is 'I' is false. In terms of the appearance, I am 'no thing'. This is why there is no objective 'I'. Or, in other words, there is no 'I'. That means that nothing that I can grasp hold of, perceive, sense or think about is who I am. But what am I, given that I am most tangibly here in some sense? We saw this before. I am the undeniable sense of presence or existence that is knowing everything or lighting everything up. It is empty or void of any form whatsoever, yet completely present and aware. This presence-awareness is known immediately and directly. No obstacles need to be removed.

Q: *But can one actually negate the false 'I' in practical experience?*

John: See what I am pointing out here and this unwinds the conceptual dilemma. The seeming false 'I' is not negated as some action or endeavor. It is seen as false, as a mere assumption. That seeing pulls out the belief in its reality. Before, during and after all seeing, you remain as that clear, present awareness.

Q: *Does simply noticing the appearance of the 'I' really cause it to disappear?*

John: Yes, because it is not there. The false 'I' is false because it is not a thing. It is an assumption. You do not negate an assumption, you simply check to see if it is true. Finding that the assumption is not true, you discover that the seeming 'I' was never present. Again, it is not an actual thing to be negated, but an assumed presence that is found, through clear seeing, to be totally absent.

Q: *Is it useful for me to ask 'Who is it that wants to know?'?*

John: Yes, that brings the assumed 'I' under scrutiny immediately.

Q: *Are my questions coming from the fact that I have not let go of the 'I', the self-centered, make-believe image I have of myself?*

John: They come from not seeing your identity with present awareness and taking the assumed separation, the imagined person, to be present and to be what you are. But it is all mind stuff floating in present awareness! You are that and you are already free. Just see the facts.

Q: *Do I do anything at all?*

John: There is no one present to do or not do. This question is driven, again, by the assumed separate 'I'! See if there is such a thing. When you see that there is no such entity at all, the question drops as irrelevant because it is based on a wrong premise. Clear seeing cuts through the fog and exposes the true position. It is not an entity or person doing the seeing, just pure knowing itself. It is not a personalized action. However, practically speaking, activity goes on quite well, but no longer in reference to an assumed self center.

Q: *Thank you for your responses. After reading my original questions several times, the answer I came to is—there is no 'I' that does anything.*

John: You have gotten to the heart it.

Q: *It would seem that I had intellectualized the whole process, like a dog chasing its tail. What happens now?*

John: Who wants to know? What ever happens now is just what appears next in present awareness. There is no one present to take delivery or worry about it. It is all a movement or display of pure presence-awareness on presence-awareness. What remains is a marvelous clarity beyond description—the truth of your own being.

## 48

## All Words Are Pointers

*Question: Can the words 'conscious-awareness' be substituted for 'presence-awareness'?*

John: All words are only pointers. There are many good ones, and they are all interchangeable. Realize that your natural sense of knowing presence is what the words and thoughts appear in.

*Q: Is being conscious of the body and sensations without thinking or labeling the same as being in presence-awareness?*

John: What I am pointing to is not a state or special sense of knowing. It is that clear knowing presence in you right now that is aware of the mind, sensations, feelings and all else. Thinking and labeling are movements in thought. Those also arise in the knowing presence. We are conditioned to focus on the mind, on the labels and judgments it generates. In doing so, we overlook our real identity as the knowing presence. Labeling and thinking must appear in the awareness itself. Otherwise, how are they known? There is nothing right or wrong about the mind appearing. It only needs to be seen in the right perspective, that is, as an appearance in awareness. We tend to overlook awareness and put all the focus on the mind. Once this is pointed out, things come into balance, and we easily recognize the fact of presence-awareness.

*Q: Is it a case of consciousness being conscious of itself?*

John: Try not to make things too complicated and miss the

sheer simplicity of this. You are effortlessly present and aware now. This is not in the mind. It is not a product of thought. The mind appears in that. Awareness is self-knowing in the sense that you know that you are. This is beyond doubt. But the thought 'I am' is not the actual I am that you are. You are present with or without that thought. Consciousness is not conscious of itself as a separate object. It is a singular presence of awareness. It is not known objectively because it is not an object. However, it is not unknown either, for the same reason—because it is not an object! Only an object can be known or unknown. It is that undeniable presence of awareness that enables you to say 'I know I am'.

# Becoming More Present?

*Question: I have noticed that as I have become more present I seem to have become more in touch with my body.*

John: Strictly speaking, you do not become 'more present'. You are presence itself. That presence is both existent and aware. That has always been what it is, and you have always been that only. It is not a deepening experience per se. It is the recognition of something that is fully present although perhaps overlooked. You could say 'as I become more aware of presence', but even that is a compromise. That is not strictly accurate either. You do not become aware of presence, for presence is awareness itself. You are that. You recognize what you are. Or you see that you already are what you are. It is the doubtless fact of being. All thought of separation from your true nature is fallacious. That fallacy is exposed. Exposing the false thought leaves you undeniably present and aware as what you are. As less interest and focus gets tied up in conceptual thought, there certainly can be a clearer recognition of experiences in awareness. There are fewer filters in place. A natural seeing and understanding comes up, even in relative life.

*Q: My eating habits seem to have changed without my thinking about changing them.*

John: There may be changes. That is the natural intelligence functioning.

*Q: This seems to stem from a greater awareness about how my body feels during and after a meal.*

John: This can certainly happen. Why not?

Q: *I have read many people who say 'you are not the body'. I understand this to mean that who we are, or our true nature, is not the body.*

John: This is the gist of it. The body is an appearance or expression within awareness. It need not be discounted at its own level.

Q: *But is it possible that more presence or less thought brings more awareness to some sense perceptions, even if they are not who you truly are?*

John: I do not have any reason to disagree with this. There is less focus in conceptual thought. This is a natural byproduct of losing interest in the apparent individual and all the false concepts based on that belief. Awareness is always shining in and through all thoughts, feelings and experiences. When attention comes out of the conceptual process, other things registered in awareness can reveal themselves more clearly.

## 50
# The Separate Self Is Removed from the Equation

*Question: On this Easter day I have been reading Chapter 27, 'What Are You Looking For?' in your book 'Awakening to the Natural State'. It got me thinking as to how I should answer that question. I think that it is to know the love of God so that I will be more loving. We have a hymn in our Methodist hymn book that contains the line 'when we can lose the love of self and find the love of God'. So my question is, is it an acceptable goal to want the love of God so that I can be more loving? Reading your statement has made me realize that rather than keep reading book after book, I need to know what I am seeking.*

John: In the end, all of the pointers get back to the same fundamental understanding. You quoted the line 'when we can lose the love of self and find the love of God'. This is the essence of everything. The belief or assumption that we stand separate and apart from the one reality or 'God' is the beginning of all doubts, fears and problems in life. To dissolve this belief is the essence of the spiritual life. Because, in truth, all that exists is that one power. That being so, where is the room for a separate individual, ego or person? Such a being is a false assumption, not a reality. Abandoning that wrong assumption leaves only the oneness as the remainder. That oneness is love itself. Love is the nature of God. Remember the statement of St. John, 'God is love'.

You mention that you want to be more loving. That approach still leaves the individual in the picture. When the emphasis is on the supremacy of God alone, the individual is no longer emphasized. God alone is. The creature is at best an instrument in his hands. When God is recognized as the only real power, then that power alone is, and that is love. Not 'my' love, but love itself. There is no longer a reference to 'I' and 'mine'. The concepts of 'I' and 'mine' are the source of suffering and separation. Without 'I' and 'mine', the cause for suffering is removed. Without suffering, what remains is the pure presence of oneness, which is God, or love.

The aim is the dissolution of the separate seeker. This is realized by inquiring if the separate seeker is even present, or else through acknowledgement of the supremacy of the one power. Either way, the separate self is removed from the equation. God or reality alone remains, the one omnipresent, omnipotent, omniscient source. That is nothing but pure love itself. As St. Francis once said, 'It is by self-forgetting that one finds'. In your true essence, you are nothing but pure love. You are not a separate person in need of attaining or manifesting love. But in shedding the false notion of separation, your real nature is revealed as love itself.

## 51
## The Separate 'I' Is the Source of Suffering

*Question: As the realization that 'I' do not exist sinks in, there is a feeling of tremendous sadness. It seems like a great loss has occurred. Everything that ever happened or will happen does not exist either. There is no joy in knowing this. There is no one here writing a letter to no one out there. Every thought, word and deed is happening on its own. So much for the concept of free will or for any other concept or belief! What possible good does it do to know this? We are all imaginary puppets playing out a part in a make-believe world. Sorry, I am venting! I do not have anyone here to talk to about this. I think the sadness stems from the fact that once you see the truth, you really cannot go back to the way things were. It is checkmate. The game is over!*

John: Sadness is a temporary mental reaction to all this. The separate 'I' sense is the source of all misery and suffering. Its removal is the end of separation and fear. What is left is not emptiness, meaninglessness and so on. That is the mind's interpretation. What is actually left is pure presence, the universal intelligence, the source of light and love, the oneness that was before the conceptual mind artificially divided things into a seeming self and other. The Hindus sages called it existence, awareness and happiness.

Be aware that the judgments and evaluations of the mind are only interpretations. They are categorically false, so do not fall for these knee-jerk comments from the mind. Stay with the simple recognition of your identity as that clear and doubtless presence. In it, you will find a subtle joy, light and peace that is utterly beyond the mind's ken. Remember 'the peace that passes all understanding'? It seems subtle, so we are apt to overlook this—just as we previously overlooked the principle of presence-awareness itself.

The mind had built its security on the belief in a separate self and on the assumption that the self was running the show. When this is questioned, it may feel like the plug is being pulled. It is in a sense. But the notion of the separate self was untenable anyway because it was the source of all of our suffering. To have it removed is for the best. The absence of separation reveals a marvelous new light and clarity. The body, mind and world are appearing on an intelligent source. Things unfold in marvelous ways previously unknown by the mind. You start to recognize a wonderful clarity and ease permeating your activities. Be willing to suspend premature mental opinions while the new perspective reveals itself. The initial evaluations coming from the mind are mistaken. See them for what they are—mere mental judgments. Awareness knows the mind, but the mind can never know awareness. All of the mind's assumptions about the nature of awareness are bound to be mistaken.

Q: *What I have been experiencing must be what they mean by the 'dark night of the soul'.*

John: Do not give that concept too much weight either! When we emphasize doubts and worries in the mind, those appear to be what is real. But that only lasts while they are taken as real. But those thoughts and feelings are illumined by awareness, that is, your nature of pure presence-awareness itself. There is no 'dark night' in awareness. When the focus was on concepts and beliefs in the mind that was the dark night of the soul! But now the reality of those concepts has been challenged and the habitual mind has lost its familiar support. Let your true nature be your support.

Q: *I feel like I have seen the promised land but have not arrived there yet.*

John: Your present true nature is the promised land. Do not hold too strongly to the belief that you are not there. It is better first to investigate what your true nature is and what the so-called promised land may be. Then you can decide where you stand.

Q: *As far as the mind's concepts, opinions, beliefs, imaginings and judgments are concerned, they usually can be eliminated by saying 'That is B.S!' or 'Prove it!'*

John: Yes, a bit of questioning or examination exposes them straight away.

Q: *There is often just silence after that.*

John: Get to know that silence. What is present in that pause? This is what we have overlooked and need to become acquainted with. What is in that silence is also in activity. Come back to the basics and verify them for yourself. All doubt, suffering and problems are created in thought due to not clearly recognizing our true nature. They do not really exist apart from thoughts, and more importantly, the belief in them. The natural state is overlooked. Questioning the reality of those thoughts and looking deeply into your true nature dissolves the belief in the mind's assumptions. The natural recognition of what is clear and present in yourself dawns.

## Objects Appear, But You Exist

*Question: When you use the term 'presence-awareness', I take it to mean that which is aware right now. It is always aware, aware of thoughts, feelings and sensations.*

John: Yes, it is a pointer to your true nature. You are present and are aware. Your presence is aware and your awareness is present. The 'presence' and 'awareness' pointers are unique because it is your real nature alone that is present and aware. All other objects are experiences or appearances known in awareness. Objects appear, but you exist. You remain steady and present through the changing thoughts, feelings and sensations. They appear as objects, but you are aware of those objects. You are the subject or ultimate knower.

*Q: That must be here, otherwise how would we have knowledge of the existence of objects? Is my understanding correct?*

John: Yes. That is simple and clear.

*Q: My identity has not shifted to awareness yet.*

John: Awareness is your identity right now. Look at the pointer and consider whether or not it is true. The conditioned, habitual response is to assume that we are something in the appearance, such as the body or mind. But they are my objects. Can I really be an object or appearance? In this way, you start to question the habitual assumptions.

*Q: I do have serious doubts about trusting my mind and placing my identity with it.*

John: Good. Now you are beginning to question the assumed identity. The whole identity with the body and mind hangs on unexamined beliefs. That leads us to take ourselves to be something we are not. It is a case of mistaken identity. The essential point is to clear up the false identity.

*Q: Intellectually, it makes much more sense to identify with the awareness than to identify with the mind. But the habit of mind seems to be quite strong. It is as if, despite it not making sense, one sticks to the belief anyway.*

John: The conditioned habits of mind have been in place from early childhood. The whole functioning of the mind is based on some of these assumptions. Our habit is to return to these beliefs as the path of least resistance. However, do not get the idea that the habits are strong or have a lot of inertia and that you are going to have to work on countering the habits and so on. They are basically a cognitive error. The error can be dispelled through clear seeing. The habits are only driven by belief. Once the true position is clarified, the beliefs are undercut. Even if the habitual assumptions arise, you now know the truth and the concepts are no longer believed to the same degree.

Habits of mind may or may not arise. You do not really have any control of that. However, such habits only appear in present awareness anyway. That stands ever free and clear and untouched by the appearances. If you try to get rid of the habits as a special undertaking, it only emphasizes the mind. It is putting the focus on the wrong side of the equation. If you settle in with the recognition of your true nature, you easily step beyond the mind. Let the mind appear or not. How can it affect you? This is what you see. Here and now you are that presence of awareness that is already free of the appearing thoughts. It is that which knows or illuminates them.

Q: *I guess I have not yet quite seen it in a crystal clear way.*

John: Come back and reconsider what is being pointed out here. Recognizing your true nature is not difficult. In fact, due to the simplicity of this, we are apt to overlook it.

Q: *Identifying with awareness causes many annoying thoughts and feelings to loose their bite. A certain stillness descends on me. But there is no big 'wow' to report.*

John: Yes. Exactly. It is good to see this. Your true nature is already present. It is not a new or unknown experience. Those would only be passing occurrences. Most people are waiting for such things, but that is looking in the wrong direction entirely. What you are seeing now is precisely what this is about. It is recognizing the ever-present true nature. As you turn to that, the concerns, worries, doubts and problems in the mind are less bothersome. It is peace and clarity, not fireworks!

Q: *It is nothing really dramatic, just a kind of a pleasant quiet feeling.*

John: As you settle in with that, you understand the profundity of what the true nature really is. This is the 'peace that passes all understanding'. It is not being 'blissed out', but rather being established in a profound depth of peace and serenity, utterly unshakable by circumstances and thoughts. How do you find this? By self-knowledge. It just takes getting acquainted with your real self. This is what you are doing in your own way now.

Q: *There is an absence of worry, though that can change in an instant when the mind throws something nasty at me.*

John: Now you are starting to see the source of the problem. Knowing the cause puts the solution in your hands. Suffering is only thoughts appearing in the mind. This is a profound insight.

Q: *When you use the phrase 'shining in plain view', do you mean it metaphorically, in the sense that 'this is so clear it cannot be missed unless you are blind'? Or are you referring to some kind of glowing sensation?*

John: The former. Your true nature is clear and present right now. When you say 'I know I am' it is not a theory. You say it because your own presence is self-evident. It is so evident that we overlook the implication of it. All the sages say 'know yourself'. Your self is that presence-awareness that is here now that allows you to say 'I know I am'.

Q: *Many of the 'enlightenment experiences' I have read about relate a sensation of seeing a very bright light. I do not believe that is what you are referring to, is it?*

John: No. Awareness is simply a clear presence of, well, awareness! For example, there may perceive light or dark, but you are aware of both. You are present and aware in pitch darkness, just as you are in brilliant light. Light seems to be a natural metaphor for this awareness. It is the presence that 'illumines' objects or reveals them. All the words are only pointers. Your true nature cannot be grasped or pointed to directly, as it is always the non-objective knower.

# Ordinary, Present Awareness

*Question: In an email to me you wrote, 'All the senses, feelings, thoughts—everything is registered or known due to the fact that you are present and aware'. Then you wrote, 'It is everyday, ordinary awareness'. For me it is hard to reconcile the two sentences. The concept of everything being registered (whether I am asleep, distracted or whatever) does not seem ordinary but metaphysical. I know it is supposed to be self evident, but not to me! Being present and aware, on the other hand sounds more ordinary and self evident.*

John: There is no significant difference in what we are talking about. Do not make this too difficult! Thoughts, feelings and experiences appear in awareness or are known. How can we cognize them if there is no awareness? Awareness is present constantly and naturally through all of our experiences. That is all I am pointing to. We are not looking for some abstract, unworldly, difficult or transcendent principle, but ordinary, awareness. Everyone can easily recognize the fact of being aware, but few really stop to consider what that really is. It is so obvious that we take it for granted. We are apt to ignore it, even though it is what allows everything to happen. Imagine life without awareness. There is not much else you can experience without it!

*Q: Thoughts do not seem to last long. Sometimes, however, the worried, anxious thoughts with their strong pull, seduce me. They repeatedly return. I feel a deep attraction to the painful ones, such as thinking about my wife's health or worrying about an unexpected bill.*

John: Those are simply thoughts. They pass like all the others. However, we invest them with a lot of value because we feel they say something true about who we are and where our happiness lies. In other words, it is our own interest in them that keeps our attention on them. Ultimately, you see that all the thoughts of 'me' and 'mine' are based on an erroneous assumption. Then the fascination, interest and belief in the mind withers away of its own accord. It is important to see the mechanism of all this. The thoughts themselves are inert and innocuous. After all, how much power or substance does a thought really have? It is like a rumor. It has little power or value unless believed in.

Q: *When I ask who is having this thought, there is nobody there, just as you describe it. But then the thought returns, though usually with less of a charge.*

John: This is a good insight. Thoughts are conditioned memories and beliefs picked up over the years. They are based on certain assumptions about who and what we are. They are often predicated on the assumption that I am a separate, limited person. But direct looking reveals no such person, as you have seen. With this seeing, the whole production is exposed, and the belief drains out of the mind and its stories. Without the self-centered beliefs, there is no more cause for being fixated on thoughts. They move along effortlessly.

Q: *Am I not investigating deeply enough?*

John: No, you are fine. See the truth of all this. The seeing is what liberates, not some imagined goal or attainment. There is no such thing, because you already are what you are seeking. Seeing through the false assumptions leaves you as you already are—present and aware. That presence-awareness is not a person, but the ground or basis from which all things emerge, their true source.

Q: *Sometimes I ask myself the old question, 'Who was I before I was born?' But my mind does not seem to resonate with that question. The mind cannot entertain the 'before birth' idea. I cannot help wondering (yes, another mind rumination!) whether I need a more incisive, deeply-inquiring mind? Despite my questions, I am not a very curious person. I have rarely asked philosophical questions of teachers until now.*

John: Do not make this too mental or speculative. Have a look and understand the basic workings of the conceptual mind and how it generates doubts and suffering based on unverified assumptions. Also, see that your natural identity as present awareness is readily known, even now. Do not imagine unnecessary obstacles or set up extra requirements to pass.

Q: *I love this non-dual philosophy. It seems to draw me, even if some of it seems over my head. I first discovered the teachings of non-duality years ago when I ran into a book by Nisargadatta Maharaj at a bookstore in San Francisco. The simplicity and clarity of your books have been invaluable in clarifying things.*

John: My case was similar. Bob Adamson helped me cut through the fog and get to the simplicity of all this. You are and you know you are. Everything else is only a passing object in awareness. Thoughts, too, arise and pass. But you are not a thought. Whatever thought says about you is not true. The whole presumption that you are a separate someone in need of help is discovered as erroneous.

Q: *The other night some painful thoughts began to seduce me. Then I read some words from 'Sailor' Bob Adamson. They reminded me that all is well.*

John: Good!

Q: *There is only one way to get out of painful thoughts—full stop! In that instant of stopping there is clarity. A second later it starts up again.*

John: All that is happening is that the mind throws up its old habits and concepts about who we are. These are false ideas that we picked up in the years of not knowing any better. What are these thoughts appearing in? Present awareness! You are that present awareness. Even now you are that. All the thoughts are false. They are based on a seeming separate person that upon investigation cannot be found. Continue to see this and the whole production dissolves. It survives only due to not investigating it.

Q: *If it sinks in often enough that there is nothing wrong unless I am thinking about it, then even if the thinking is going on, I do not have to take delivery of it. That is the cause of all my problems. So I can let the mind go! It is that simple, so simple that we miss it. I can stay with the subtleness, that silence and stillness.*

John: Keep up this looking and seeing. Let these insights guide you back to your own direct seeing and knowing.

# 54

## You Are Awareness

*Question: I can be aware, and thoughts mean less than they used to. I feel a sense of relief, but the awareness is too ordinary, it seems. There is awareness. So what? There is no particular bliss or sublime peace. I am a little stuck. Can you help?*

John: It is not that 'you' can be aware. That divides something that can not be divided. You *are* awareness. You are constantly that. That is the necessary ground from which all arises. What can there be without awareness? Everything arises and sets in awareness and has no independent existence apart from it. That is the substance of which everything is made, including you. It is you. That awareness is pure peace and happiness because in it there is no separation, no isolation, no fear, no past, no future, nothing to obtain and nothing to lose. Separation, fear, suffering and problems arise in the mind due to the notion of being a separate someone apart from the wholeness. When that notion is examined, you find it is false. This seeing undercuts all the erroneous dualistic thoughts in the mind, and you return to the direct knowing of oneness or non-separation—not that you ever left that, but the conceptual fog is removed.

The conceptual mind says that awareness is ordinary. That is because the mind has no cognizance whatsoever about this. In seeing all this, you discover—non-conceptually—that awareness is the one and only reality. The non-conceptual understanding of your real nature as present, clear awareness or pure non-conceptual knowing is actually quite a marvelous and extraordinary thing. Be willing to look and see what that might be. Do not judge too quickly. Last time I checked, all the traditions that I am aware of had some pretty good things to say about discovering your true nature!

# 55

## Doer-ship Arises in the Question

*Question: I have a question for you regarding a statement in one of your books. I have the impression that what is being stated is, inherently, a message of ever-present awareness. I am puzzled, though, as to how to interpret the introductory comment on page six of 'Shining in Plain View': 'The reader will be delighted ... to see how this understanding unfolds and becomes direct experience for those who apply themselves with earnestness, follow the pointers ...'. The phrase, 'for those who apply themselves' brings to mind 'doer-ship'—as if 'a somebody' could exert effort in the interest of understanding true nature and thereby make progress in realizing it. What was the intention here?*

John: All pointers are relative and to be dispensed with ultimately. You cannot say in words or point without bringing in something objective. You are right. The answer is ever-present awareness. If that is clear for you, you do not need to consider other pointers. You do not need anymore pointers or books. For those for whom this is not clear, the suggestion is simply to consider this fact. That is all. No doer-ship is implied. Have a look and see what is being pointed to. There is no need to bring in a reference to a doer. Because, as you are seeing, there is no such separate entity in the picture.

Right here and now, you are what you are seeking. Seeing this, the search is done. Why search or ask questions when you are already that? If this is clear, then the need for teachings and pointers is finished. If it is not clear, questions are bound to arise and various pointers are given to point you back to the essential nature. There is nothing passive about this approach. The questions come up, pointers are given, they are verified and the understanding arises. As I always say, the approach that 'all is oneness, so there is nothing to do' is a bit of a stretch because that is often an intellectual statement for most people. However, on the chance that this is truly a lived understanding, there is no real issue because then there are no doubts, questions or problems, and there is no dilemma.

You can try to steer clear of all apparent dualism in words, and some try to, but it is completely hopeless because all language is in the manifestation and dualistic by nature. Even a teacher like Ramana Maharshi would say 'hold on to yourself'. Who, why, how if you are that? Nisargadatta Maharaj would say 'go in the direction of the sense of I am'. Why, if I am that? Buddha said 'work out your salvation with diligence'. Why, if there is no one? However, these are expedient pointers given in particular circumstances. Some say everything is presence, but then talk of awakening and final liberation. Why such talk if everything is already that? Others say all is predetermined and enlightenment will or will not happen. Why, when there is no one and everything is that? You see, all these pointers lapse into contradictions. That is why they must be taken very lightly. They are tools to be used and discarded.

The saving grace is that words are only words. They are symbols not the things in themselves. There is no non-duality in language. The moment you open your mouth, there is apparent duality. Anyway, this is all words. You are present and aware and that is all this points to. Everything else is a concept arising and setting in clear, present awareness.

Q: *The desire here is to craft language so that there is as little room as possible for a 'me' to grab onto.*

John: Who has the worry or needs to craft anything to eliminate any footholds for a 'me' if there is no such thing? See that there is no me at all, then all is finished in that seeing.

*Q: In this regard, I was not addressing 'pointers' in general, but rather a specific turn of phrase, that is, 'those who apply themselves with earnestness'. As I perhaps did not state clearly, this sounds to me like a 'directive' or 'prescription' aimed at achieving a result. This phrase is received as a support for 'I' identification, rather than an undermining of it. Does this make sense?*

John: No. In practice, people seek teachings to resolve doubts and questions, are given pointers, consider them and see the true position. Seeing that all is one and there is no separation, all the doubts are resolved. It works like a charm and is perfectly successful in actual experience, and has been for thousands of years of apparent time. Ramana Maharshi gave his teachings to inquire into the Self. Nisargadatta Maharaj gave his teachings and advice, much of it in the form of directives to look, understand and question. This is because the trouble or suffering arises from a cognitive error, a lack of clear seeing of the true situation. Advising someone to look, question, inquire or consider the facts is simply encouragement to question the cognitive error that is being believed in. In a nutshell, the seeming someone is encouraged to look and see if the seeming someone is real and if any separation from source is true. So what if it is given in the form of a directive! That is encouraging us to have a look and see the true position. If the pointer is followed, the truth of it is realized and the interplay between the seeming speaker and listener is over with.

The real issue here is—are these basic pointers clear for you? If so, then the doubts, worries, concerns and sufferings based on imagined separation are no more. That is something you must look into yourself and acknowledge one way or another. For myself, I was familiar with the theory of this for many years. Yet the personal suffering and sense of being a seeker was still in force. This was resolved through personal contact and interchange with someone who knew for certain his true nature. Many directives, suggestions and encouragement were given, which I gladly followed, based on reason, faith and direct experience. The result was dissolution of the belief in separate individuality and the undeniable recognition of the fact of our nature as non-dual awareness.

It is good to be precise in language, but also make sure that the essential points are thoroughly understood so they are your direct experience. Real understanding does not occur at the level of language. Language is in the mind. Your true nature is utterly beyond the grasp of thought. The answer is not in the mind.

*Q: I guess it boils down to an issue of semantics—and yet, this personality is keen on that!*

John: Forget the personality! Words or no words, you are. That 'you are' is the key.

# 56

# Residual Doubts

*Question: John, I cannot help sending you thank you notes. There is a deep sense of gratitude here. Thank you for all your support. Getting direct feedback is very effective. I feel very lucky. Were it not for you, I would have written the whole thing off as insignificant and just continued to search. On top of all the other feelings, there is some confusion such as 'What is going on?' 'Can this be true?' 'Am I kidding myself?' All of these are not a real problem, though. I also noticed some subtle arrogance developing. Yesterday, at the meeting, I pooh-poohed another participant's questions, writing them off as merely an attempt of the mind to stand in the way of understanding. While this may be so, my behavior was somewhat insensitive. Whether it was productive or not, I do not know. It may be that I need to keep these things to myself for a while until I get a better handle on things. I need absolute clarity, not merely sparks of understanding supported by your communications.*

John: The mind is bound to throw up residual doubts and questions. This is par for the course. After all the years of living from those perspectives, they surface from time to time. There is nothing wrong with that. After all, the appearances in the mind do not disturb the fact of your existence. What are all these questions arising in anyway? Can they be there without your own nature, your own sense of existence and awareness? Seeing this, you can relax with things and go with the flow of whatever happens to appear. No harm done!

Arrogance is comprised of thoughts and feelings driven by old beliefs and concepts in the mind. So, exactly as it is happening, those are seen and questioned. They are naturally discarded if they do not serve any particular value. If something needs to be seen or re-evaluated that will come up. There is a natural and innate intelligence within us. That has brought us along quite well so far and will continue to reveal whatever is needed.

The result of seeing what is clear and present within us is that the belief in separation and the attendant concepts and beliefs lose their charge and unwind naturally. It is not really a goal, but a side effect of seeing the true state of affairs. There is no real benefit in turning it into a goal, because you are already your true nature. It is a settling in, so to speak, with something that was here all along but overlooked. Even that is a way of speaking. It is a pointer. The recognition of all this starts to dawn and you know it for yourself. Part of it is, I would say, coming to trust your own experience and direct knowing. When you let go the focus on conceptual thought, a natural peace and clarity is there. This is not a theory but known by immediate experience.

# 57
## I Am Already Here

*Question: A few weeks back, I was hit by the realization that this is what I have always been looking for. It has always been here. It was fantastic. But as thought gets involved and you start thinking about it, you lose sight of it, or so it seems.*

John: Now you are seeing the essence of it. That is the beginning of the end of being taken in by the mind. Your true nature is always present and clear as the doubtless sense of being that allows you to say 'I know I am'. Thoughts come and go, but only because they shine in the presence of the one awareness that you are. The fascination with thoughts keeps us—for a time—looking away from the obvious presence of awareness. Once you begin to question the mind, you easily step outside of it and take up your stand as your true nature beyond the mind.

*Q: I have been questioning the 'I', as you and others advise. Although I could not see it before, it all unfolds by itself. What else can it do? Ha ha! I find, when I look, that what is right here and now is awareness. Of course. I am already here.*

John: Excellent!

*Q: It seems difficult, though …*

John: But is your actual presence or the fact of being aware difficult? Not at all! Do not get the idea that this is difficult, because is not. It is so easy that we overlook it.

*Q: The difficulty seems to arise because the mind is still trying to grasp it, but there is not anything to grasp. There is no reference point, nothing to hold onto. The mind tries to step in and take charge.*

John: Yes, but this doesn't have anything to do with the mind. The mind appears in awareness but cannot know awareness. It is the wrong tool. Give up looking in the mind or relying on the mind. Set that aside. You are and you know that you are. This is not recognized in the mind at all. It is a non-conceptual, direct knowing. It is very, very easy indeed.

*Q: In the empty stillness, there is nowhere for the mind to stand. It has a real problem with that. But then you let go, the mind sort of shuts up and goes off and sits in its corner.*

John: Once you see that your real nature of presence-awareness is not even in the mind, you stop looking there. The whole relationship with the mind relaxes and you let it do what it is good for—handling relative affairs. It is almost totally useless for knowing your real nature. See this and you will naturally and effortlessly stop relying on the mind.

*Q: But there is still the apparent problem of it all being so elusive. It is difficult to relax into this, when there is nothing to relax into! I could go on and on in linguistic circles, but I am sure you can see where I am. You have probably been there yourself once upon a time. It is all so funny and ridiculous. I have got it, but haven't. I feel so close, but so frustrated. Do you have any comments on any of this?*

John: Your own being or awareness is clearly, easily and naturally evident. It is not an attainment or acquisition. It is not even something to relax into. All those are misconceiving the matter. You are present and aware, correct? You know that, correct? That is it. That is what you are. Frustration comes in because we think this is something that we do not have.

But this is wrong. See this error and the frustration drops. You are what you are seeking. Everything else is a passing concept or thought arising right in this present awareness. It is that simple. If you continue to turn back to the mind for confirmation or direction, you will seem to move away from the simplicity of this.

*Q: There is another problem I am concerned about. Some people have a problem with their kids or family and how this will affect their life and so on. For quite a few years now, I have been interested in and involved with the Western mystical tradition, which involves magic and mysticism.*

John: This stuff is mostly at the dualistic level. Much of it is based on the subtle belief in the reality of appearances, time, individuality, superior powers and so on. In its higher forms it points toward non-duality to some extent. But why not go right for the recognition of oneness and avoid detours?

*Q: I still have many goals and desires for my development along these lines, various psychic or metaphysical abilities and so on. There are many things I want to work on. I found my way to non-duality through its mystical side. I first found Wei Wu Wei's books, then Zen, then various contemporary authors. But I am afraid that any desires or goals in pursuing magic, studying it, enjoying it, will disappear.*

John: They may or may not disappear. But who is there to care when the individual dissolves and all there is is oneness and peace? You also see that the appearance is only that—a mere appearance arising in consciousness. At best it is a manifestation of consciousness. But, more accurately, it is really non-existent because all there is is consciousness. There is nothing to seek, attain or develop. Magic, occultism, powers and so on are all founded on the belief in the reality of the appearance and one's existence as a separate entity. They tend to inflate the belief in these things, rather than diminish it. The vast majority of followers of these approaches get stuck at the dualistic level and never get around to realizing their true nature. At some point, you may want to consider whether you are pursuing powers and abilities, which are only relevant to an individual wielding them—or if you are pursuing the approach whose sole aim is to utterly dissolve the separate seeker. As you can see, they are founded on almost contradictory premises.

*Q: You are clearing up some things. Some of it I had seen already, though I got diverted. You said some things about magic I hoped you wouldn't! But I know much of what you say is true. But what if, for example, aspects of it are considered as hobbies or interests? What if they are enjoyed for their own sake, like any other interests? Couldn't such thing continue as interests after the 'me' has gone, just as other aspects of one's life can go on unchanged? I am coming from the point of view of sheer curiosity and delight in the whole thing itself. Also it wouldn't hurt to be able to nudge things to my advantage if possible! A lot of this is from a non-power position. But if I said there was not any idea of power in it, then I would be kidding, too.*

John: There is no prohibition on doing anything. Who is there doing it anyway? I am only pointing to some possible pitfalls to consider. Your own native intelligence will guide you. It is all the one power anyway. Stick to the basics and let the appearance unfold however it will.

## 58
## There Is No Need to Fix Yourself

*Question: Thank you for the consultation. As I was driving to work the next day, I realized how easy it would be for someone to think that they exist and that they are aware. I had said this myself for years. As I was sitting at the beach pondering our session, I realized how many suggestions came out about how to see my emotions. That has actually lifted a lot of pressure I felt in dealing with them. I had not really been aware I was carrying that around. There is a greater sense of freedom now.*

John: The belief in the need to 'deal' with emotions brings in the involvement and ownership of them, which is a needless burden. It is much more effective and effortless to simply see them for what they are—passing appearances in clear, present awareness. The need to manage them or fix them comes in from the residual belief in separation, that one is separate and defective in some sense and that one needs to do something to be all right. But none of this is true. It comes in from a mistaken belief in a false identity. By letting your identity return to the perfection that you already are—pure presence-awareness beyond the body and mind—the belief is undercut at the root and there is no need to fix yourself. This seeing undermines the conceptual house of cards and the emotions come into a natural sense of harmony and appropriateness.

# 59

## Do Not Turn This Into a Project

*Question: When thoughts appear relating to the 'I' sense, I investigate them. Of course no 'me' is found. I place attention on the feeling of 'I am', but sometimes this feels like an effort, which I feel is in contradiction to being natural. I feel a conflict between witnessing thoughts, staying with 'I am' and the fact that it is not relevant if the mind is busy or not. I realize that presence-awareness is something always there, not something to be achieved. I feel I am overcomplicating things for myself. Can you clarify this for me by pointing out how staying with 'I am-ness' should be done?*

John: You say that you see that there is no 'me' to be found. Good. Then you go on to say that you subsequently place attention on the 'I am'. This is where you take a wrong turn. Who is doing this and why? This is going back into conceptual thought, based on the idea that I am separate and need to do something. Why pick up this thought? Seeing there is no 'me' is the end of the line. If there is no 'me', then who is separate, who has a problem and who needs to do anything? Picking up those concepts only troubles the mind with needless seeking. If there is no 'me', then all you are is that present awareness itself. That cannot be denied, 'me' or no 'me'.

At some point, you see that it is needless to return to the mental reference points. You are present awareness. It is clear, open, natural and effortlessly present. Be what you are, and forget the mind. You have seen there is no separate 'me'. Stop there. Do not step back into imagined separation and give credence to thought based on the imagined 'I'. If you take this to heart and see the point of it, you can 'throw in the towel'. You are what you are seeking and no separation has occurred.

The pointers are only to verify this. Do not practice it. See the truth of it.

One other point. Do not struggle with the mind. The mind is only passing thoughts. These are only waves or emanations of awareness itself. It is only awareness appearing as thoughts, so nothing is disturbed or lost. The coming and going of thoughts does not disturb your nature as awareness in the least. Everything that appears arises from and returns to this. Everything is only the fundamental awareness itself appearing in the form of seeming objects. Things cannot exist as independent entities apart from awareness, so they must be that in essence. So all there is, is one awareness shining in all directions and at all times. Here and now, you are already that. See this and be at peace.

*Q: Your answer made it clear to me where I was taking a wrong turn. I was going back into assumed separation after seeing that there was no 'me'. I was attempting to turn abiding in the natural state into a practice! Thank you for pointing out my misunderstanding.*

John: You are seeing this now. Do not turn the natural state into a practice or a maintenance state. All that might happen from now on is that the mind occasionally produces self-centered concepts out of habit. No harm. Let a gentle seeing expose that. Return to the simple and direct knowing that you already are what you seek. Nothing can be simpler than being what you are. From here you will see all attempts to know, stabilize and pursue are still driven by assumed separation. In that seeing, any remaining belief in the notion of assumed separation is resolved conclusively.

## Awareness Is Always 'On'

*Question: There is a recognition of the constant presence, which is always 'on', so to speak. There is no need to look for it. It is all effortless. Thoughts may arise and start telling the story in this presence, but they subside gently without bothering anyone (who?). All objects, including thoughts and the body, are seen as perceptions. Sometimes the upper part of the body disappears. In this presence, the so-called 'I' comes up. When looked for, this elusive 'I' associates itself with certain body sensations, such as inside the head or in the throat, trying to make believe that it is something existing inside what we call the body. It is like chasing a phantom.*

John: I am happy to hear that the basic understanding is settling in. You now see what you are—effortless, ever-present presence-awareness. You are right. That is always 'on'. We have been living in that, as that, from day one. We've only overlooked it. Everything else is an object appearing in this. There is no separate 'I' as such. It is only a notion. That notion appears to survive by associating itself with various appearances—body, mind, personality traits or whatever. The very fact that the 'I' sense constantly shifts from one thing to another proves it has no real basis. It is like a ghost with no body of it own. When inquired into, you see that there is no such entity. You are not a separate, limited entity. You are pure awareness itself. This is utterly free and unconditioned by the body, sense and mind. However, those continue to act quite well in response to circumstances.

## 61

# The 'Me' Is the First Illusion

*Question: Following our correspondence, I was in a mindset of thinking that the recognition had happened and then somehow disappeared. This was because thoughts and feelings came in. It was dramatic, and I seemed to get lost in the dream, forgetting what I am. You clearly pointed out that these were only habits. The momentum perpetuates for awhile, but at no time am I not 'that' while all this is happening.*

John: Yes, that is the gist of it!

*Q: I really get that now. I see that no matter what seems to be appearing I am always the same—this presence-awareness. I now understand your direction to me to just be and not to try to think about it.*

John: Good! You are understanding the fundamental point!

*Q: I am seeing that there is no person here, no 'I'.*

John: This is the clincher. If there is no 'I', there is no one left. All problems and doubts hang on the assumption of a separate someone.

*Q: Without getting long winded, there seems to be a deepening of the understanding, even as I know that that is not possible. It can only be here and now. And it is. It is! The sensation that seems to go with this I would have to describe as gratitude, a subtle vibration of joy, for no reason. These are labels and cannot really describe reality. What word or concept could possibly describe this?*

John: There is no need to describe it. But I understand!

Q: *I now see that it is the 'me' that is the illusion in the first place!*

John: This is such a key insight. It unwinds the entire basis of all misunderstanding, doubt and suffering. I am glad that has become clear for you.

Q: *It is amazing to me that throughout our entire lives, we have never questioned our identity. We only took the false as true.*

John: It is very good to see this.

Q: *Questioning the reality of the 'I' seems a radical thing to do, and yet it happens. Then this seeing or understanding comes to the forefront. It was always there, but unrecognized. What a wonderful happening, this aliveness, this presence, whether it is recognized or not!*

John: Beautiful. This insight leaves you with the clear and vivid sense of your true nature, whatever you want to call it—life, light, clarity, joy, presence.

## Books Come and Go in Awareness

*Question: I have been nose deep in your books. I could teach it by rote memory at this point. There are more insights, more joy, more glimpses of no-self. It feels like there are no escape routes at the moment.*

John: Books come and go in awareness. Without awareness, how many books can you read? The essence is already clear for you. No amount of reading will make this any clearer. Question the idea that you are not there yet, that there is something to get or understand, that someone has something or some knowledge that you do not. You have the full and complete understanding of this already, no doubt about it. You know everything that anyone else knows. Trust me. Trust yourself.

All you are dealing with is a few residual ideas like 'I am not there yet', 'In the future I will stabilize', 'I am something other than present awareness', 'Someone else has it' and so on. Resolve this once and for all. Ask yourself, 'Here and now, am I anything apart from pure presence-awareness?' If you are not, then what type of realization or understanding do you need? In truth, you need absolutely nothing—no understanding, no realization, no deepening, no final understanding. Those are all concepts that have outlived there usefulness. You are already what you are seeking. Present awareness is all there is and you are that. The idea that you are apart from that is only an idea. That single, unassuming idea triggers all the seeking and suffering. No amount of experiences or reading will ever resolve that. Those are all looking in the wrong direction. Simply look and question that assumption. If you are not separate from presence-awareness, which is the one and only reality, then what could you possibly need to do, understand or acquire? This is only a restatement of the basics that are already clear for you.

*Q: I must be comparing my current state with my previous state without realizing it.*

John: Consider the following points. You are present and aware. All that can possibly appear is an arising right in this that you are. Without that presence of awareness, nothing can be. It is the ground and source of everything. As things arise and pass, you remain as the changeless sense of knowing presence. That is your real nature. Look and see that you cannot possibly say that you are separate from that. The conceptual mind is predicated on the notion that I am a separate individual entity. All desires, seeking, suffering, judgments and evaluations of who and what we are, are predicated on that notion. But there is no separation from the source, as you have seen. There is nothing beyond awareness, because all experiences, attainments and states only exist because they appear in awareness. Look into this until it is clear that you are not a separate, limited entity at all, but the space of knowing presence from which everything arises. Jane, the one who did this and that, went here and there, needed this and that was only a fictional character in a story imagined in the mind. There never was such a one, nor can she be found now.

# 63

## There Is No Expansion into Awareness

*Question: The following quote seems to sum up what is key for me right now: 'Avoid forming any more opinions about this. Simply see and know'. That is from Gilbert Schultz's writing, but I am sure you have said the same thing many times. When I spoke with a friend on the phone this morning, she was stating something about feeling into awareness because then it expands and so on. I am seeing for myself that that is a subtle carrot.*

John: There is no expansion into awareness. Awareness is fully present and clear. Your identity as that is not approached or deepened into. It is only confirmed as fact. All those gradual approaches are founded on a presumed separation from awareness, as if it were some type of goal that is not present. Those concepts are fallacious. They can be dispensed with by reviewing the basic pointers and confirming them in your own experience.

The only seeming separation is the mind's unfounded concept that we are apart from that. But how can anyone be apart from their own existence? Seeing this, all the remaining concepts are seen through and naturally discarded. Nothing is added or gained in the process. There is only seeing what is clear and present but may have been overlooked.

All seeking, getting, stabilizing, studying and approaching is based on the belief that I am separate from that, that I exist as some kind of concrete substantial, limited entity apart from presence-awareness. In direct looking—here and now—no such entity can be found, much less your identity as such a thing. So it is all an unfounded, illusory conceptual position formulated in thought. Where is that thought arising? Right in your present awareness. Recognize your inescapable identity as that. Just look at and discard any contrary concepts. The seeing undercuts any residual interest in the conceptual mind and leaves you as you always are—clearly present and aware and non-separate from the one presence that is the basis of everything.

You do not deepen into what you are. You are what you are. The person created by the mind and all of its beliefs and attributes are not your actual identity. You are not a thought, a person or an entity. You are the empty space or clear, knowing presence in which all appearances and possibilities arise. This is 'no thing' to the mind, because it is not a tangible, objective thing that it can grasp. Yet it is clear and present as that which enables you to say 'I know I am'. It is doubtless presence and awareness.

## 64

# Start from the Position that You Are Already Free

*Question: I have to admit that the frustration is great. I do not know what to say even. I know I have to stop, but it feels like if I stop I will go back to business as usual.*

John: Why not take a step back and look again at the big picture? There is one and only one source, one reality, one essence. Its nature is presence and awareness. These are not distant, metaphysical entities floating 'out there', but reside within you as the undeniable sense of knowing presence that allows you to know clearly and beyond doubt that 'you are'. That is constantly present as the background of all knowing, feeling, sensing and perceiving. It is not to be grasped, attained, understood, approached or stabilized into. Those are all imagined, based on the assumption that you are separate and apart from that presence-awareness. Thoughts and feelings of frustration, of imagining that 'I' have to stop, and doubts about what will happen in some imaginary future are based on notions such as:

- There is something I do not have.
- That the answer is something apart from what I am.
- That I am a limited, separate person.
- That there is a future time in which I can attain some thing I do not have.

But the facts are actually:

- There is no reality 'out there' apart from you.

- You are what you are seeking.
- You are not a limited, separate being at all.
- Presence-awareness is what is real, and you are not separate from that.
- The future is purely imagined in present thought. It does not exist as such.

The mind is generating some thoughts and concepts and a bit of credence is given to them. In short, they are believed. That is like putting a ball and chain on your leg then trying to walk. This is not about stopping anything. That is dualistic and emphasizes the imagined separation. This is about seeing the true position, seeing what is going on. You are feeling hamstrung by residual concepts and suffering over them. But you are continuing to hold onto them and give them value. You cannot stop the beliefs by some act of will. Who wants to anyway? That is more mind stuff! That is the mind falling back into the same games about a poor, separate person who is in need of some thing that is assumed as missing.

This is not about a great enlightenment, a mystical experience that happens. Not at all. It is not about getting something or stopping something by an act of will. It is seeing a few basic facts and questioning residual beliefs and concepts that generate dualistic thinking. The sense of frustration is only showing that the separation from presence is still assumed as true. Can you see that?

See the thoughts and assumptions in the mind and get them out for inspection. You have already seen what your true nature is, but you are stepping back into the mind and trying to find some more answers. Why not put your energy into seeing, really seeing, how the mind is generating dubious and fallacious concepts and some lingering belief is going into them. The net result is that thoughts are given more attention than the clear, shining presence of your true nature. There is no answer in that approach. It is an endless cycle of trying to find answers based on the mind's false premises. See this and the whole mechanism stands out as clear as day. Start from the position that you are already free. If you look at the mind from that position, the belief in thoughts cannot be sustained. They are all based on the opposite, erroneous premise. In truth, the basics are clear for you in a very profound sense already, but it helps to get reminded and thrown back into the lived recognition of this until it is inescapable. Then any remaining doubts or conceptual positions are exposed once and for all.

# 65
# Dealing with Practical Matters

*Question: I thought I was doing very well here of late until the last two weeks. I dealt with the break up of a long-term relationship and worked through it pretty well. Seeing it as a movie on the screen of awareness has been helpful and, of course, trying not to identify with this 'self' I perceive me to be. I received a letter from the tax revenue service wanting to do an audit on my taxes for the year 2001. All that would not be so bad, except for the fact that I have lost my records! I am experiencing a great deal of fear. Nothing seems to help. I am trying to just be with it, see it, notice it and so on. It is more than unsettling. It is really getting to me. Any advice would be greatly appreciated.*

John: Have you talked to a good tax person to see what your options are? In a situation like this, the mind can generate reactions due to not having a clear sense of the options available. If you talk to a competent tax person they may be able to alleviate your doubts and concerns and point to some reasonable options. If you and your tax person come up with a reasonable strategy, the mind will likely settle down around this issue. This answer is not too flashy, I admit! I am an advocate of taking appropriate relative steps. The same goes with medical issues, job issues and so on.

In terms of dealing with it from a spiritual perspective, you mention being with the feelings, seeing them, noticing them and so on. It is interesting that you have discovered those approaches do not work very well, if at all. That is a good lesson. One thing you did not mention was understanding them. Why are they arising? What are the assumptions they are based on? What is the mind imagining might happen?

What is the mind saying about you? How does all this tie back into the mind's definition of who and what you are? What is the image of yourself in play here?

Situations are impersonal. They cannot generate fear of themselves. However, the mind may find in them an excuse to throw up its conceptual ideas of who and what we are. It is those self images that are the real source of the trouble because we take them as true even though they are counter to what we really are. Those ideas can be seen and understood to the roots. You will find that in all suffering states, there are some core notions or ideas about our identity at work below the surface.

## 66
## Simply Being What You Are

*Question: It is like I never looked at any of this. There is not any particular point that I do not get or do get. I do not see the big deal, especially with the giddiness some people express.*

John: In some sense, it is no big deal at all. It is simply being what you are, and realizing that things are simply as they are. The suffering, seeking, doubts and problems in life are unnecessary, because they are based on a cause which can be cleared up through understanding. Perhaps there is uncertainty or doubt about ourselves and the nature of the world. Those too can be effectively resolved through understanding. Sometimes these issues never even come up for consideration, or there is simply no interest in them. Then, there is no real point in looking into it. There is nothing particularly flashy or exciting about this. It is more of a calm, clear and simple consideration of the facts of who and what we are. The result is clarity, simplicity and peace. This is the residue left when the mind is no longer spinning in doubts, fears, questions and seeking. I like Nisargadatta Maharaj's statement: 'There is nothing wrong anymore'. No giddiness is implied in that, as far as I can see.

## No Awakening Is Needed

*Question: The clouds already broke up long ago and the sun shone clearly for no one. Awaiting awakening is simply a lingering confusion in the mind. There will never be an awakening. It is the concept 'me' who thinks the conceptualized oneness will awaken. What a fine concept! The 'awakening' already happened! To no one. It appears now as an event but only from the mind's standpoint.*

John: All sounds good. The basics are there for you and clearly known. All is seen, known, understood and expressed from the clear, knowing presence that you are. 'Me' and 'awakening' are only words! The 'me' is not. Awareness is. No awakening is needed because there is no 'me' present who can awaken and your essential nature of aware presence is the very space that all happenings appear in. Presence-awareness is not an event. You cannot even say there was a moment when it became known. Only objects can become known. Awareness is not an object. It is the ground from which all knowing arises. You cannot say it is unknown because only things are known or unknown. It is simply the undeniable fact of pure being, ever present and ever aware. Looking reveals that you have never been separate from this. It is not an attainment, but a recognition of a timeless fact.

*Q: Some things are still a mystery, such as whether awareness is still intact in deep sleep or under anesthetics. All I can say now is that all, including any sense of existence, disappears in those conditions. So, it seems my feet are still tangled in some concepts which support doubt.*

John: Every doubt or question, as you know, is a ripple in thought, which itself stands illuminated in clear, knowing presence. If such a thought troubles anything, it troubles only another thought. One thought may link to another and another, but they are all motions in the space of knowing presence. That cannot be lost due to the play of thoughts. How could it be, when those passing thoughts themselves depend on your true nature, awareness itself, even to manifest? Awareness remains untouched, untroubled and uncompromised at all times, regardless of thoughts.

Waking, dreaming and sleeping do not disturb your essential nature. There is no troubled mind in deep sleep, only peace and refreshment. There is no question raised from that state. The thinking process is in abeyance in sleep. It only evaluates that state of sleep later, but not from the sleep itself. The mind is not qualified to raise doubts and questions about sleep, because it was not present there to gather any information! All the conclusions it comes to regarding that state are hypothetical. The doubts and concerns are simply present thoughts. In the moment of their occurrence, we can attend to the thoughts or simply notice the clear presence of awareness shining here and now. Then present thoughts cease to disturb us because their impact fades in the light of awareness. Sleep is peace and rest and needs no comment. Why stir the pot and create a problem where there is none? That is typical of the conceptual mind—to generate a problem where none existed previously and then take the problem as something significant and worthy of attention! The same old story!

Q: *I seem to be waiting for the next bout of doubt and unbearable suffering.*

John: Know that whatever may come can only be a few thoughts and ideas. From the position of present awareness these are never a real disturbance. They are only ripples passing through the clarity that you are. So there can be no disturbance, unless we overlook what is clear and true and give all the belief to passing concepts. Seeing all this, the potential to suffer diminishes and becomes impossible. The key is to focus not on the thoughts or possible thoughts, which are insubstantial, but on the clear presence of awareness itself. The sun does not care what passes through the sky. Awareness does not care what appears within it.

*Q: The paradox that arises in the condition of the suffering 'me' is this. When I stand as awareness, there is no room for psychological suffering. While, when there is psychological suffering, awareness is supposed to be untouched and free.*

John: Continue to dismantle any lingering separation between 'I' and awareness. A separation is introduced where there is none in reality. Continue to recognize that in all states, all thoughts and all feelings, awareness, your real nature, remains present and undisturbed. It is not 'supposed' to be free and unaffected. It is. How many thoughts, even suffering thoughts, can you have apart from awareness? None. Awareness does not disappear or waver. We think it does, but this is an illusion. All the focus goes on thought and the ever-present awareness and our identity as that appears to be overlooked. However, looking into this clearly reveals the true position.

At this point you can dispense with making a division between thoughts and awareness. That is good in the beginning as a means to make awareness evident. However, from another angle, thoughts, feelings and perceptions arise from, exist upon and subside into awareness. They have no real substantial or independent existence apart from awareness. So they are only awareness appearing as those forms, like waves emerging from the sea. It is all one substance. There is only one awareness, one presence. There is no separation possible, because there is no division in reality. There are no objects in ultimate truth, only awareness. There is no one standing apart from that. Everything that seems to appear is only that. All thoughts and feelings are only that. All is that. You are that. So what can you gain or lose at any time?

*Q: Those doubts I mentioned are mind-boggling! Again, this thought is probably more than a little twisted!*

John: It is only a passing wave arising and setting in clear awareness. Nothing is gained or lost.

*Q: In general, there are no problems right now. There may be a few clouds here and there.*

John: The separate self has never been. You, as clear, space-like, empty awareness are totally, completely free and have never, ever been in bondage!

# 68

## The Simplicity of Presence-Awareness

*Question: Today was very busy. There was some frustration over dealing with practicalities, but it did not take me into suffering. However, there are some doubts. I no longer think things should be different. I have seen through that one. Maybe all doubts fall into that category, ultimately. But it seems like I am doing fine and then slowly I slip into mind traps before I even know what has happened. On the other hand, I feel like the seeking has stopped for good. I absolutely see that it is nothing more than this simplicity. I do not think I can lose that.*

John: The habit is to attend to thought, as if that is the way to peace. Well, check it out! Does it work? Keep your eye on the fact of being, the awareness. That is where the sweetness lies. It is in the utter simplicity of pure, doubtless presence itself. Eventually we get the simple point. Following the mind leads to confusion, problems and doubt. Remaining with pure awareness, the sweet sense of 'I am' without words, drops us right into peace itself. Touching that peace, all the concepts, even spiritual ones, turn to ashes. Peace does not need experiences, understandings or awakenings. Those are like soggy socks served for a Thanksgiving meal. Stay with simple peace and presence. It is not an attainment. It is in the simplicity of here and now. You need nothing because you are that.

*Q: I see the simplicity. That is so clear. In the middle of all this 'stuff' there has been simplicity and peace. And boy, it is nice. Going with the mind is not peace. There is no controller, no decision maker. That arises with the mind, but disappears in simplicity.*

John: You are seeing this clearly. Continue to be with what you know, with what is simple and certain. All the awakenings, investigations, readings, comparisons, getting it and all such things will lead you back into concepts. Everything the mind tends to say is based on 'I am not there'. The reason is that the mind has no cognizance of simple presence and peace. It is like taking for your tour guide a self-styled expert who has never even visited the location in question! The real destination is always in the here-and-now. This does not mean in the mind or objects, which, after all, are only passing appearances. It is in the simplicity of pure presence, pure being, the knowing presence behind the thought 'I am'.

What is it that enables you to say 'I know I am'? That is the wordless knowing of simple presence. Settle into this. It is the real source of peace and joy. It is never found as an attainment, experience or future state. Fall back, recede, merge into simple being, pure presence-awareness. No thinking or special spiritual acrobatics are required to be. It is there in every moment as the constant presence in and behind all appearances. The mind cannot know this, but you can because you are not in the mind. What you are knowing is what you are.

Do not think, study or fret about this! Easy does it is the way! Go about your life in a natural and normal way. If it is a help, simply notice the fact of being. Take some time to notice what is present and aware. Get to know that, make friends with that. We have been giving all the attention to the mind. Our own nature deserves a bit of attention, too! When the focus falls away from the mind, the clarity and certainty of this is known, wordlessly and non-conceptually. It is only simple being. The awareness of being is peace or happiness.

# 69

## Doubts Are Thoughts in the Mind

*Question: I have written to you before about my doubts.*

John: Doubts are thoughts in the mind. They come and go, but you remain. Why attend to doubts, when your own nature is clearly in view?

*Q: I have been focusing on the sense of self.*

John: This is a way of speaking. You and the 'self' are not two things, one to focus on the other. You are that self itself. Just take note of this fact.

*Q: I know that the body, feelings and thoughts are manifestations of the whole, but the presence is still there. The presence is required to see the manifestations.*

John: Correct.

*Q: I have become a little distant from my desires and wants.*

John: This is fine because they are only appearances. They do not affect your true nature. As you settle in with the clear knowing of what you are, the interest naturally falls off of passing content in the mind.

*Q: There is a little detachment. I have become disinterested in most of the things. I have stopped reading books or buying toys and gadgets, which I used to enjoy. I find emptiness in all of these things. For example, I had always wanted to travel abroad, but now I find that to be useless and just a lie generated by the mind. I know that even after buying the gadgets or toys or going for a world tour I will remain the same and the happiness derived from these things will not last more than a few days.*

John: The clear perspective makes itself known. There is not and never was any genuine happiness in those things. We thought there was! This does not imply scorning or abandoning appearances at their own level. That would be overlaying a negative judgment from the mind. Appearances are meaningful at the level at which they appear. Engage in them and make use of them at the appropriate level. There can still be a relative enjoyment and interest in things. Why not? Nothing is lost or gained.

*Q: The problem is that I am still frustrated that I am not getting it. I know that this frustration is also an appearance in the awareness.*

John: It is based on a misunderstanding. The answer is your own true nature. It is here and now. Why the frustration that you not 'getting it'? It is based on a misunderstanding of what 'it' is. So have another look and probe a bit deeper. Frustration arises in the mind when we think there is something we do not have. How does this apply in the case of being yourself?

*Q: I read that I can only get this understanding if I meet a live teacher. Otherwise not. Is it true that a live teacher is required to get this understanding and that books do not help? Can people keep struggling for years and not get it if they do not meet a live teacher? I hope that this is not true!*

John: You are what you are seeking. There is a residual concept in play that there is something to get 'out there' or that there is some special future understanding. Neither of these are true. Seeing this, the problems drop away. They are based on a misconception.

*Q: I have read about everything being impersonal. My seeking, doubting and frustration are all impersonal. The seeking is happening, the doubting and frustration are happening, but no one is doing it. It is happening to no one.*

John: This is all right as far as it goes. It is a popular catch phrase. But it is an approximation of the true state of affairs. All those things are arising due to the assumption of a separate one, that is, that you exist apart from the oneness. They go on as long as that position is believed. If you accept those experiences as true, the underlying root cause is still present. Get to the root concepts. That is the most effective way.

*Q: I have heard it said that when someone gets the understanding that it is also just happening, and it is not happening to any one.*

John: This shows how convoluted people can make this when the basics are not clear! No one gets any understanding. That is still based on the assumptions that there is a separate self and that there is something apart from us that we do not have. Both concepts are false. Scrutinize the premises and come to a clear view. Then the whole problem resolves quite nicely. The seeming problems are driven by false premises and cannot be resolved as long as those premises are assumed as valid. It is subtle, but really very simple. Can you get a sense of what I am pointing to here?

*Q: How do I see the truth and get the understanding?*

John: See that the truth being pointed to is the fact of your own being. It is not an attainment or understanding in the future at all. See thoughts as thoughts and relax the focus on them, since they are incapable of yielding any peace. Be what you are. A simple, natural and clear peace emerges as you recognize your present identity as being and awareness. Being is effortless. Notice what is present and let go the concepts of attaining and getting. Once you see this, it becomes much simpler. Your own present being is the source of all understanding and peace. You have everything you need right within you. No further understandings are needed or required.

## 70

## What Good Does This Do Me?

*Question: You point to the sense of existence. But what good does that do me?*

John: It is a pointer to be followed, investigated, explored—not something to stand back in judgment of. That would be like standing on the shore of a lake on a hot day and saying the waters are refreshing—but never diving in.

*Q: I know that I exist. But it seems so useless.*

John: This is a prejudgment, rather than a direct experience. The trouble is that we have been conditioned to put our trust in the conceptual mind. We are inclined to put all of our faith in its conclusions. But the mind is completely incapable of understanding or recognizing the significance of the non-conceptual recognition of being or awareness. What does the mind know anyway? Why put so much emphasis on these ephemeral conclusions from a witness who has no experience of what it is talking about?

*Q: I intellectually know this is the key to unraveling the false ideas of the 'I', which is the source of suffering.*

John: That is a start. It is like saying, 'I intellectually know the path to the well, but for some reason I am still thirsty'. You need to see the truth for yourself. This is not an intellectual endeavor at all. Using the mind may be a start, but the refreshing water is not in the mind at all.

*Q: But the ideas do not unravel!*

John: Because you are not actually looking. There is a lot of thinking, but not much application! When the implications of what is being pointed to are really understood the motivation to look is there. This may also arise when the suffering and doubts are no longer acceptable.

*Q: Because I know suffering and problems have a stop, and because I consult my feelings and do not feel that they have stopped, I hope and expect for something in the future.*

John: There is nothing in the future because the future is an imaginary concept, not a reality. You do not find yourself by looking in the future. You find yourself by looking away from the things you wrongly take to be yourself. You look for that which stays clear and present in all times and states—your own sense of being and awareness, which cannot be denied under any circumstances.

*Q: The thought comes that I should practice self-inquiry.*

John: This sounds good, but it is misconceived. This is not a practice at all, which is only a superficial regimen conducted by the mind. That is like a man holding a red hot iron poker saying he should practice dropping it. This whole topic should grab you full force by the throat because you realize that it holds the key to your suffering—and happiness.

*Q: But the sense of pure presence-awareness is so ephemeral*

John: This statement is the complete reversal of the facts. Your presence-awareness is the one rock-solid and clear factor in all your experiences, feelings and thoughts. How many of those can you have if you are not present and aware? All of those arise within and depend upon your presence. Everyone knows 'I am'—no one can doubt it. Yet we assume that our own being is somehow absent. Wonder of wonders! All of the doubts are based on the seeming non-existence of awareness, yet those same thoughts cannot even arise without awareness. They are utterly dependent on it for their very presence.

Q: *Thoughts very quickly hijack the investigation.*

John: So it seems, but that is where the clear understanding and recognition of the origin, sustenance and workings of the mind are immensely helpful. There are several ways to tackle the mind and its distracting thoughts:

- See yourself as the witnessing presence of the mind.
- See that thoughts point to the fact of the consciousness in which they appear.
- See that they arise and set in awareness and are made of awareness, like waves are made of water.

My sense is that the mind has been your main tool for navigating the seas of life. It is what you are mainly turning to for your understanding of things. You must clearly understand the limited role the mind plays in self-knowledge. The right tool is presence-awareness itself because that is the only thing in our experience that stands beyond the mind.

# 71
## Drop the Analysis of It

*Question: Am I aware? Yes. When I answer this question I notice that there is a looking to objects for verification. The objects point to the fact of awareness-of-objects. Perhaps this is what Franklin Merrell-Wolff meant by consciousness-of-objects? Do I exist? Yes. When I answer this question, I do not refer to any objects or thoughts. So there is knowledge-of-existence. We could also use the term 'awareness-of-existence'. Perhaps this is what Merrell-Wolff meant by 'consciousness-without-an-object'? Awareness-of-objects is fairly easy to grasp because objects point to it. Awareness-of-existence is immediate, but then the mind begins to question it, presumably because it is beyond the mind. Mind is an object in awareness-of-objects. When you said this is what Nisargadatta Maharaj was pointing to, did you mean awareness-of-objects or awareness-of-existence, or is this a false distinction created by my overactive intellect?*

John: As I see it, your nature can be pointed to as either existence or awareness. Both mean the same thing. That is not an object at all. Yet it cannot be denied, because everyone knows 'I am'. I am not talking about awareness of objects. For lack of a better term, we are talking about awareness of awareness, or in your terms awareness-of-existence. It is the same pointer. It is that in you which allows you to say 'I know I am'. In spite of its seeming intangibility, it is the most solid and clear factor in your experience because that must be there for anything else to appear. Without you, nothing else can be. Drop the analysis of it and recognize in immediate, non-conceptual experience the fact of pure presence-awareness. It is not difficult. It is so simple that we discount it. Besides, the mind has no cognizance of what we are talking about anyway.

# 72
# When the 'I' Is Not, There Are No More Troubles

*Question: I went inside and tried to find 'Mary'. It was so clear to me that there is no one in there. That feeling is clear to this day. Anger comes up but it just floats through for a while and drifts away. This morning hurt feelings came up. They also floated away. I remind myself that I exist right now. This part of the understanding is not as easy as knowing for sure that there is no 'Mary' in there. Right now there is the frustration of not seeing what is so simple. I would appreciate your input on this.*

John: You see that there is no one there. What is present and knowing that understanding? That itself is the pure presence or being itself. You know you are present and aware. It is simple and much easier than we think. It is the simple knowing that you are. You can see this immediately. That simple sense of knowing is all that is being pointed to. Do not make this too difficult. There is nothing more you need to know, attain or understand. Relax and be what you are. It is natural and effortless. When the 'I' is not, there are no more troubles, so do not drum up any unnecessary ones!

# 73

## The Suffering of Others

*Question: Thank you for your books. I come to these after some years in the Dzogchen teachings, as well as those of Nisargadatta Maharaj, and having spent time in the essence of mind. Experientially, that is as incontestable and undeniable as you and all my teachers have said. When I read your books, as with Nisargadatta Maharaj or the Dzogchen texts, I can bask in the resonance. My use of the word 'I' is for convenience only. I do not mean to suggest an independent entity. There has been something bugging me for a few weeks. I do not know if you saw the Greenpeace report last week? Deaths from the Chernobyl disaster were more likely to be 93,000 than the official estimate of 4,000. I have a friend and colleague in whom one can palpate the radioactivity when he is suffering from radiation sickness. There are photos of all this on the Internet. They are utterly horrific.*

John: Every living form that comes forth in the world of appearances will perish eventually. This is an inexorable law. That demise may be through old age, disease, accident or any other cause. In some cases, some bodies are instrumental in the demise of other bodies, either accidentally or intentionally. Intentional destruction of living beings may be done due to ignorant and ignoble intentions or, sometimes, wise and noble intentions. It is hard to argue with any of this, given that this is what actually occurs. I am not condoning or evaluating any of this, but stating things as they are. As you know, I distinguish between pain and suffering, pain being a bodily or organic reaction to some stimulus. In short, bodies feel painful and pleasurable sensations as part of their functioning capacity. None of this implies suffering, as I use the term.

By suffering, I refer to interior doubts, problems, worries, concerns, fears and conflicts arising in the mind due to false causes. In this context, I am referring to those causes rooted in the mistaken sense of identity, specifically, taking oneself to be a limited separate self. This type of suffering can be eradicated through clear understanding, which removes the root cause of ignorance of who and what we are. That is to set the stage for how I would approach this.

*Q: My doubt is about the fact that my being in the natural state does not change any one else's pain or suffering.*

John: This brings in a false duality. You are not a being who is in the natural state. You are not a being, a person, an entity at all. This is, in fact, the root confusion. Nor are there other separate selves, ultimately. That again goes against the basic point. Of course, I understand what you are saying practically, but you must understand that by inadvertently letting in the assumed separation between self and others, the root cause of suffering is maintained, though under an altruistic guise. Suffering, anxiety and problems are inevitable in that conceptual framework. The suffering or doubt is not 'out there' in the experience of supposedly other beings, but 'in here' in the very mind raising the doubts.

*Q: I do understand that as far as 'my' involvement in this goes, there is not a 'me' to suffer or agonize over the sufferings of 'others'.*

John: Yes, true. But do not leave this theoretical. Are you saying that the seeking and suffering are over in fact, or only as a possibility?

*Q: It goes right back to the Boddhisattva question. How can you be happy in nirvana when other beings are suffering?*

John: First, there is no 'you' to be happy in 'nirvana' (assuming nirvana to mean peace or freedom). This would be a misinterpretation, in my view. The understanding is that the 'me' does not exist, so there is no one in 'nirvana'. Then the sense of 'others' is also seen as a concept. All apparent others are only appearances arising in your mind, not actual independent and substantial beings at all. Even if they appear to suffer, it would be for the same reason that 'you' appeared to suffer—the false belief in being a separate self. As your suffering is not ultimately real, but based on a misperception, neither is theirs. What is the compassionate and clear response? To point to the root of suffering and its resolution. You cannot do this unless you have experienced it yourself. Otherwise, it is the blind leading the blind. In other words, as Nisargadatta Maharaj said, you yourself must be beyond the need of further help to put others beyond the need of further help.

In seeing the basics for yourself, the self concept is removed, and you no longer make a distinction between self and others. In practical experience, there is simply a movement to alleviate suffering out of natural compassion when possible to do so, without any calculated program or viewing oneself as distinct from others. Keep in mind, as mentioned above, the whole world is an appearance in your own consciousness anyway. What plan do you have for eliminating suffering of those beings perceived in your dreams? Ultimately, this is what it gets down to.

*Q: All the traditions confront the issue of evil at some point, either by saying the person affected brought it on themselves by sin, karma or even evolutionary choice, or that the evil and the suffering are both illusions. I understand that these are only concepts, but they sure do not help very much. I would not wish that kind of suffering for those infants and their families.*

John: So-called evil derives from not knowing your true nature. All suffering and doubt comes from this.

*Q: From the Buddhist perspective of interdependent origination and non-dual vision, I see that I am part of this situation, and I am also not separate from the people and the activities that created this.*

John: Yes, but not as a separate entity. When the separate entity is questioned and dispensed with, there is no basis for separation. All is seen as it is—an arising in the one awareness that you are. You are not one with those things, but they (as pure awareness) are identical to what you are in essence.

*Q: That is comforting as well as sobering. I can also see that whatever I choose to do about this or any other source of pain and suffering is fine as long as I do it from the natural state of presence awareness.*

John: No, you are missing the point. You do not exist. You as a seeming separate person, doer, entity or agent are not and have never been. You are not. That is why without this being seen, there will always be insoluble riddles and thorny issues. The fundamental premise is erroneous.

*Q: You partly answered this in your book, by pointing to the fallacy of object as well as subject. That is also undeniably accurate. But it still, well, sucks!*

John: This is a judgment coming in from the mind and not a clear view. Ultimately, there is no independent appearance at all, no separate beings, no real basis for suffering. To quote: 'All there is is non-conceptual, self-shining, ever-fresh, presence-awareness—just this and nothing else. There is nothing other than this'. In this, there is nothing wrong at all. Belief in the solidity of the appearance, separate beings, suffering and all dualistic concepts emerges from an unexamined or incomplete view of things.

*Q: My question, though, is—is there any point, value or merit in the presence of awareness while this is going on?*

John: Yes, without this understanding, there is the appearance of endless doubt, suffering and separation. Buddha called it the endless cycle of birth and death. Presence-awareness is the nature of reality. Your nature of presence-awareness is freedom itself—the ultimate truth of emptiness and awareness that is the heart of all non-dualistic teachings.

Practically speaking, realize your own true nature first. Without this, it is all speculation, however noble. Then you will be in the best position to help others out of their own suffering. But then you will have a much deeper understanding of others and their suffering. There is no denying the appearances at a practical level. This is not nihilism. Do what you can to help as the opportunity presents itself. The best help is your own realization of your true nature. Without that, it is all half measures.

## 74

## Something Clicked

*Question: Something 'clicked' for me. I saw that awareness is not a mental construct, and for this reason it is trustworthy. Understanding that awareness is not a mind function has made a difference. Thank you for hanging in there with me on that one! I also noticed how I was holding onto some assumptions about the descriptions of awakeness by other teachers. Those concepts appear to have fallen away into a greater, yet no less discriminating, openness. Does this make sense? I find it valuable to hang out with apparent persons who do not reinforce the idea of separateness. I am very grateful for your generosity.*

John: I am glad something clicked in for you. We often overlook the very basic and core point of all this. There is a principle that stands free of the mental constructs and projections of the mind. It is the essential reality of what we are. Looking from the mental constructs, we overlook this. From that position, we can never recognize who and what we are. Taking a fresh look, we can recognize present awareness or the fact of being itself. This is clearly evident and yet often unnoticed.

Let the focus fall from the identity posited in the thinking mind and return to the fact of your actual presence and all of this becomes immediately clear. This also undercuts the root of all suffering, seeking and doubts. These are always traceable to a confusion about our real identity. That is the essence of it in a nutshell.

## 75

# Materialism, a Faith-Based Religion

*Question: You have talked about present awareness a lot in your books and the falseness of any spiritual search.*

John: Yes, because the goal is your own nature. How far do you have to go to get there?

*Q: My question is a very silly one but one that has bothered me for sometime, since I am a materialist.*

John: I am not sure what you mean by materialism, but if it is that matter alone is real and there is nothing beyond that, how does one absolutely know? There is always a possibility that new evidence may be uncovered, so the position is more of a hypothesis, really. But then, so is religion, idealism or any other 'ism'. Like all the other 'isms', materialism is a faith-based religion! As far as I am concerned, they are all on equal footing. Each one takes a partially verified belief system and states it as absolute truth! However, there is another approach, which does not rely on unverified assumptions. It moves by directly verifiable experience. Neither believers nor materialists actually do this, because at some point they end up asserting a belief as incontrovertible truth.

Materialism as a metaphysical position is far from bullet proof. Like any other metaphysical system, it has its strengths and weaknesses. But they all do. That is why there is no finality in metaphysical speculation. It is always subject to doubt. That is why Buddha and others would hardly even talk about metaphysics. It is all conceptual and open to revision. It is often pointed out that the answer is not in the mind. Once you understand this point, all interest in metaphysical systems fades, because they are creations in the mind and have no real substance. You say that you are a materialist. This happens to be a point of view you adhere to at the moment. You are something quite different from a belief system in the mind!

Q: *How do you know that your present awareness is not merely a deep metamorphosis in perception or even a physical or biological change?*

John: Awareness is not concerned with appearances and changes, be it body or mind states. All thoughts, emotions, states and objects appear in awareness. This is not speculation, but seen in direct experience. However, it is not to deny that there is not a deep shift of understanding or perspective involved in this. Of course there is! The whole problem is based on a cognitive error of believing ourselves to be something we are not. That is clearly an erroneous belief resident in the mind. This belief is uprooted through investigation and clear seeing. However, the principle of awareness itself shines clear before, during and after such investigation.

Q: *I was bothered by the fact that there seem to be genuine teachers who had Alzheimer's disease or senility in their old age. I would not be worried about cancer as it is a physical illness. However, the losing of one's mind to senility or Alzheimer's, despite deep realizations, is deeply disturbing to me.*

John: Why on earth would this be disturbing? Diseases and disabilities strike the body, brain and other organs. The functioning is impaired. What of it? Senility or Alzheimer's are debilitations of the brain and nervous system, as far as I am aware.

Q: *It indicates that all the realizations are in one's physical brain rather than a direct perception of reality, because there are teachers who literally became idiots in their old age.*

John: Not at all. It only demonstrates the failing of the instrument of expression. If your hands are crushed, you cannot do much with them, can you? You do not say 'I am my hands; therefore if my hands are severed, I cease to exist'.

Q: *As a scientist, I really cannot come to terms with the radical realizations.*

John: Why are you so concerned with radical realizations? Nothing of the sort is needed. All such realizations are only passing, transient experiences. You will make more headway if you forget about such things.

Q: *Whatever they are, such realizations seem to be some sort of perceptual or physical change, rather than a direct insight into the nature of reality.*

John: There is only one thing pointed to as reality, and that is your own real nature. Is that anything physical or mental at all? Awareness is a fact. Every object of knowledge or experience demands the presence of awareness to be known. Awareness knows thought, but thought cannot know awareness, being an appearance in it. The lesser cannot know the greater. The bottom line is that the body, senses and mind are not the right tools for approaching this. If you always rely on those, you cannot get to the heart of the matter. At some point, you must leave the mind behind. It is useless for the non-conceptual realization of awareness.

You cannot deny the principle of awareness. It is self-established and needs no proof. It must be present for any proposition to be made. You can debate and talk about awareness for eons from the mind level, yet the living experience of this will appear distant. All speculation is futile. To approach this, you must relax the focus on the mind and its endless insoluble riddles and puzzles. Those only generate doubt and anxiety. Immediately, you will notice a certain lightness, ease and joy emerge. There is no need to speculate about this and attach to it any metaphysical position at all. Such will be more mind stuff. This is the direct acquaintance with your actual present nature. As you get acquainted with this, you will see that the state of pure being or knowing remains constant in all states and experiences. This is entirely beyond the mind and must be approached non-conceptually and immediately. Then all the pointers will become clear in direct knowing, not as speculation.

# 76
# Presence-Awareness and Perceptions

*Question: I want to clearly distinguish between presence-awareness and what are merely sense perceptions.*

John: These are quite different. Sense perceptions arise and set. They come and go. They are known by you. You are that presence or awareness knowing them. Even when sense perception is not happening or not noticed, you do not disappear. There is quite a difference, really. On the other hand, sense perceptions cannot exist apart from awareness. How many sensations have you had without awareness? None! Sense perceptions never exist apart from awareness. They cannot be anything other than that. Keep in mind that sensations are only an expression on awareness, like waves on the sea. The sea continues whether there are waves arising in it or not.

*Q: In one of your books you wrote 'It is easy to distinguish between awareness and ideas ... see that awareness is clear, vivid, alive .... It is the continuous sense of registering or knowing of all that appears. Ideas are only images, ideas or words arising in awareness'. Here is the part that is not clear for me. The registering of all that appears seems to show up in terms of sense impressions—colors, sounds, images and so on. These sense impressions seem to be immediately translated into ideas (for example, 'the ocean is beautiful').*

John: Yes, but only when the conceptual process starts. That is an overlay on pure perception. All the 'trouble' starts in the conceptualization process. In pure perception, there are no problems, no concepts, no separation and no duality at all.

*Q: Presence-awareness feels like it is inextricably linked to these sense impressions—as if it is the same as them.*

John: You are, whether sensations appear or not. This is undeniable. Your true nature is not a sense impression. They arise to you.

*Q: It is as if presence-awareness is being mistaken for all of these sensory impressions! It feels like I am getting caught in an illusion here. Is there anything you can say to offer some clarity?*

John: It is only sensations appearing and disappearing in present awareness. Who is caught? What is the problem? Do clouds disturb the sky? Leave them alone and they pass right through every time!

*Q: I want to move on to the issue of self-identity. It is quite clear intellectually that there is no separate self. Yet, when the body hurts, immediately the identification seems to draw itself back into the body-mind—as if 'I' am the same as this body-mind that is experiencing pain.*

John: It is only sensations arising. Why refer them to a 'me'? And where is such a 'me' anyway? Did you ever find one? The body appears and disappears in awareness. It is an appearance like any other. Calling it 'me' is only possible after the conceptual process starts. Otherwise, how do we know it is 'me'? But you are there before the conceptual process starts or even before the body as such is perceived.

## 77
## You Are the Answer

*Question: At last there is difficulty in continuing to read your words! The words you have shared through books and your web site have been the final answer leading to the elimination of the need for more and more answers. There is now an understanding beyond the need for words, an understanding that silently describes the truth.*

*At forty-three I am feeling the wonder of life as a child again. But now whenever the childlike question 'why?' arises, the answer always comes from knowing rather than thinking. There is a realization that all of the questions and answers are simply contained in the play of presence-awareness.*

*The 'why?' requires no answer now. There is simply a sense of relaxation into the simplicity and awe of being. There is no more need to be impoverished by grasping onto the idea of a tiny false self when the infinite is our true inheritance. There is a realization that this treasure is our natural birthright. It can only be grasped with open hands because we already are the wealth we seek. Thank you for sharing so many clear pointers to the truth.*

John: I am pleased to hear that you are having difficulty reading my words! At some point along the way, the pointers must be left behind, just as one must set aside the menu and eat the meal. The pointers in books and on websites are a double-edge sword. Being words, they can lead one right back into the mind. However, if your intent is freedom and you have the willingness to look beyond the words, then they can give us a bit of a nudge.

Your words ring true and show me that your own understanding of this is alive. You know where the answer is. You are that answer. Ultimately, there is no other answer beyond seeing that what you are seeking is what you are. The separation from source never occurred because you are that source. The separate self, the root of all suffering and doubt, is a myth. It is a conceptual error that is directly resolved by clear seeing. This you have done. Now the direct, immediate knowing is awake in your heart.

From here, personal suffering and problems lose all their hold. Nothing can touch the empty yet vividly present 'no thing' that you are. Do not hesitate to pass along the pointers as the opportunity arises. This is one thing that you can share with full knowledge and confidence—because what you are sharing is what you are.

*Pointers*

# *Pointers*

Our true nature is not a new state or experience that will arrive in the future. It is already present, though we may have overlooked it. It has been called awareness, existence, spirit, essence or the heart. It is simply what you are, that knowing presence that is the basis and support of all thoughts, feelings and experiences and their manifold expressions. We have been looking elsewhere for the answer, yet it has been right with us all along as our own true nature.

What could be simpler than being present and aware? It is totally effortless. The fact of our being and its nature of awareness cannot be doubted. Try it! Even such a doubt appears right here in clear, doubtless awareness itself. Acknowledging our identity as this presence of awareness, a clarity and joy naturally reveals itself. From here, life unfolds as a spontaneous expression, without reference to a limited, separate person. It is the natural state.

In the end you see that the mind's questions are based on imaginary problems. Even the question 'Why did ignorance ever arise in the first place?' is a last attempt by the mind to grasp onto a doubt, rather than simply acknowledging the clear and certain presence of the heart. No harm. Nothing is lost or out of place. The questions come up, but they must all dissolve back into this undeniable clear light of knowing and being. You are what you are. This cannot be doubted. Being is. Awareness is. You are that and nothing but that. Not in the future, but now. It is simpler than we ever imagined. Know this and live in the peace and joy that are your natural birthright.

Awareness is undeniable. Otherwise, you would have no cognizance of anything. In your direct experience can you find any separation between yourself and this undeniable awareness? For example, is awareness an object appearing to you? You will see that you cannot possibly see yourself as something apart from awareness. So awareness is a characteristic of your fundamental nature. The characteristics of your true nature are existence (or presence) and awareness. Your being or presence is aware and awareness exists—it is. In direct looking, you do not stand apart from this. Further looking shows that awareness is 'no thing'. This means that it is nothing that can be perceived by the senses or thought of by the mind. It is that to which those appear. So awareness is no thing or empty by nature (in relation to appearances). Looking like this clearly shows that your fundamental nature is presence, awareness and emptiness—simultaneously. These are not different things, but only different ways of framing in words the same basic experience—the fact of your true nature. Furthermore, it is not something distant. It is vividly present and clear. It is unchanging through all passing experiences. Verify this through direct looking—right now. In your true nature, there is no suffering, doubts or problems whatsoever. Those, should they happen to arise, are characteristics of objects, such as body, senses or mind. But they are not characteristics of awareness itself, which is what you are inherently. So your true nature is peace itself, oneness itself. It is whole and complete as is. In itself, it is ever-present, unbroken clarity and joy. It is a constant radiation of clear presence, vivid cognizance and unbroken peace. Look deeply into what is being pointed to and verify it for yourself.

Before the next thought, feeling or perception arises, you are. That 'you are' is what this is about. It is your true nature. Look directly into this and see what you discover. What can you say about it? First, it must necessarily exist because you are undoubtedly here as the one to whom thoughts, feelings and perceptions appear. And you are aware. Right now, this aware presence must be what you are. Experiences come and go, but this true nature remains constantly present and completely untouched. It has no observable beginning or end—therefore, it is beyond time. It has no edges or borders—therefore, it is beyond space. It has no form or shape—therefore, it is beyond birth, growth and death. It has no doubts, questions, fears or problems—therefore, it is beyond suffering. Your true nature shines throughout all states and circumstances. It is present in waking, dream and sleep, without any break or change. The world, body and mind appear in it like clouds passing beneath the sun. It is a solid mass of pure, radiant presence-awareness that is ever-present and completely undeniable. You have been fully one with this from the start. Since you are not separate from this, it need not be approached, grasped or attained in any way whatsoever. It is. No practices, techniques or time are required to see this. There is absolutely no need to deepen, stabilize or embody the recognition. Those are redundant concepts, since you are already completely one with your true nature right now. All is full and complete.

The past is gone, the future has not yet appeared—both are completely non-existent. The external world of forms and objects is only assumed. All we can say for certain is that we are aware of sense perceptions. But these are experiences arising in the mind. On present evidence, there are only thoughts, feelings and perceptions passing through awareness. Only one thought appears at a time. There is ever only awareness and one thought. What is the nature of a thought? It is fleeting, insubstantial, ephemeral, weightless, hardly present at all. It is a ripple, a movement, a vibration passing through awareness. What is it made of? Since it arises from and subsides into awareness, it is nothing but awareness appearing in that momentary form. Try to grasp hold of a thought and you come up with nothing substantial. Attempt to look at it and it vanishes in the very act of cognizing it. So there has never been an actual thought present. No thought has ever existed. There is awareness alone—nothing else. The world, the body, the mind, the assumed individual and his suffering are appearances in thought. But thought does not exist. It has no substance or independent nature at all. So there has never been any bondage whatsoever. All there is, is undeniable presence-awareness. Right here, right now, you are that.

Under no circumstances can you deny the fact of your being. Thoughts and experiences come and go, but you—as that presence of awareness—remain. Thought does not create you or define you in anyway. Your own presence is what all the thoughts appear within or upon. No attainment or special state is required. It is noticing something so clear and evident that we may have overlooked or discounted it. The simplicity is the key, really. Be as you are and let the thoughts and feelings flow freely. Do not grasp them or push them away. Your true nature cannot be denied. It is effortless presence-awareness. That is shining in plain view at all times.

Your true nature is the undeniable ground of all appearances. It is not something to seek or achieve. No change in the content of the appearance (thoughts, feelings, experiences) is necessary to recognize what you are. It is that bare sense of pure presence or being itself. It is not inert and lifeless. It is alive, aware, cognizant. Being is aware, and awareness obviously exists. Being and awareness are two terms for the same thing, your true nature. And that is 'no thing', because it cannot be grasped or objectified by the mind or senses. Yet your true nature is clearly present because you can never say 'I do not exist' or 'I am not aware'.

If you can say 'I exist, I am aware', then you definitely recognize present awareness. Have a look and notice that your own direct experience of being present and aware is utterly beyond doubt. Simply pause and be. Any expectation, evaluation, judgment, comparison or analysis will be stepping back into the mind—a subtle moving away from present awareness. See that this movement is never conclusive because you are trying to find an answer or confirmation in the mind. But the answer is not in the mind. As long as there is interest in the thoughts and stories of the mind, the interest goes there and the natural peace is overlooked.

The external events of life cannot touch your true nature, just as clouds in the sky do not touch the sun. The sun stands ever free and untouched, no matter what goes on below. In exactly the same way, all thoughts, feelings, events and situations appear and subside right in present awareness. That is what you are. That is never lost, clouded over or compromised at any time. How can it be, when it is that very presence of awareness that is knowing all of the thoughts, feelings and experiences?

Awareness is. That is what you are. It is neither dualistic nor non dualistic, those being further divisions in the conceptual mind. All teachings, concepts, objects, bodies, thoughts, states, feelings and so on are only momentary appearances in awareness. Any label applied to awareness is simply another appearance in awareness itself. All objects rise and set in awareness. They have no independent existence apart from that. Because they are never experienced apart from awareness, they must be awareness. So all there is, is awareness. Nothing else, in truth, is. There is no separate, independent self at all. That is purely imagined. And from that concept comes all suffering, doubt, seeking and problems in life.

All doubts, worries, concerns and problems arise in the mind and only exist when they are being thought about. One solution to this is to try to silence the mind, but the very attempt is another activity of the mind and creates more mental turmoil. Even if the mind is temporarily suppressed or absorbed in some state or experience, it is bound to give trouble when it activates again. In response to suffering, most of us either seek happiness in experiences or attempt to silence the mind. Experience proves that neither of these approaches yields lasting satisfaction and peace. So the answer must lie in another direction.

The most important point is the fact that you are. Being is. And being is not only present but brightly aware. It is that presence that allows you to say 'I know I am'. That is the positive knowledge of your true nature. From there, you can see that you do not stand separate and independent from that at any time. So the separate, independent person is only assumed, but not actually present. We miss this, not because it is difficult but because it is too simple. Rather than grasping the simplicity of it, we tend to go back into the mind looking for complications and more work to do. The mind thrives on time, distant goals, difficult accomplishments and drama. Remember, this is about the natural state that is shining in plain view. Right here, right now, it is the seeing of your true nature as present awareness.

Enlightenment, awakening, self-realization and so forth are all empty concepts. Speaking of such things keeps us seeking for something we think we are missing. Presence-awareness is here and now. It is clearly in view for everyone, though perhaps overlooked. There is no deepening or future expression. Such notions keep the assumed separate entity in full swing. There is no before and after awakening, because there is no awakening, no entity and no time. These are all concepts. There is only what is, here and now, and you are that and nothing else. From here, all attainments, stages, levels or deepenings simply evaporate into thin air or, rather, into ever-present awareness.

Silence and activity are two sides of a dualism. They are both simply expressions in the appearance. Your true nature of awareness, being or presence shines out full and clear in both silence and activity. It is as much present in the thick of activity as in moments of silence. Do you not exist in both states? If this point is not clear, we may mistakenly seek quietude, assuming it to be a more 'spiritual' state.

Waiting for the 'I' to drop away is a delusion. There is no 'I', so how can it drop away? There is only a simple noticing that what is here is only presence-awareness and that there is no separate one apart from this. Seeing this, the belief in the existence of the independent 'I' is cancelled.

All suffering, doubts, questions and problems are appearances in the mind. They are simply thoughts and feelings about a seemingly limited, deficient, separate self. The belief in the existence of this separate self and the subsequent identification with this concept is the root of all of the self-centered thoughts and feelings. The concept of the separate self is the cause, and the self-centered thoughts are the effects. When you investigate the separate self, you discover it is absent. The plain truth is that the cause of suffering does not exist. We have been suffering, seeking, doubting and questioning due to an unexamined concept, a false belief, a conceptual error. Resolving this error through clear seeing brings freedom from the suffering, seeking, doubts and problems of the separate self.

Awareness is not an attainment. It is what you are. Meditation or any other practice cannot bring you to awareness. You are already present and aware, even before you have any thought or intention to do anything. Awareness is not a personal state that comes and goes. The notion of being a person is what comes and goes. It arises and sets as a flow of conceptual thinking within awareness. The notion that awareness is a transient personal state that arises and passes away is false. Awareness, your natural presence or being, is present before, during and after any and all states or activities. Awareness is perpetually and effortlessly 'attained' for everyone at all times.

If you try to think about your true nature or grasp it as an experience, it appears to slip through your fingers. All it is, is the simple, clear and undeniable sense of being present and aware. It is the sense within you that allows you to say 'I know I am'—nothing else. Though it is not an object or experience, it is undeniably here. If you doubt it, then look right now and see that your true nature is here. It must be here. Any residual interest in the self-centered stories in the mind keeps us looking away from the sheer clarity and immediacy of presence-awareness. Always come back to the fact that you already are what you are seeking.

With the belief in the existence of the seeker exposed, what remains is peace, which is synonymous with happiness or the end of suffering. Snapping the belief in an entity that was never present is the end of suffering because the cause of suffering is the belief in the separate 'I'. Like awareness and being, peace, or the freedom from suffering, is not an attainment or goal. It is the natural condition of what is.

&

'Enlightened beings' are fine as far as they go, but they are still appearances that come and go in the only real light there is—your own awareness. People search for enlightened ones, not realizing that they could not even appear without one's own being. So being is the source. It is like speaking of the radiance of the moon and not realizing that the moon has no actual light. In this case, those speaking fail to realize that they themselves are the light that is illuminating all experiences. Imagine the sun, the only source of light, speaking of the radiant moon! You are that unwavering 'I am' at the root of all thoughts, feelings and experiences. All else is a passing experience, which cannot be there without your presence.

&

Thoughts, feelings and experiences appear and disappear before you. But you never disappear. Your true nature remains as the knowing space containing all appearances. What is the nature of that presence? It obviously exists, for you are present. It is also aware, for you know all that appears and disappears. Your true nature has no problems, worries or suffering, so it is peace or happiness itself. Recognize the immediate and wordless presence of your true nature in direct, non-conceptual knowing. With this seeing, it is evident that the limited person you took yourself to be does not exist, except as an assumption. When this is understood, suffering, doubt, seeking and personal problems vanish entirely. They only survive as long as we believe ourselves to be a separate, limited self. But there is not and has never ever been any such thing as a separate self or person at all.

༄

Your natural being is not contained in or even known by the mind. Seeing this, you stop looking for an answer where it cannot be found. You are present and aware now. Pause thought and simply be. Notice that there are no doubts, problems or suffering unless you are thinking about them. Seeing this, you stop chasing thoughts and concepts in the mind. You simply relax, knowing that you cannot be anything but that presence-awareness itself. That is incredibly clear, vivid, alive and open. See it for yourself.

༄

Clarity and joy do not actually come and go. Erroneous conceptions based on an assumed separate self arise in thought and the attention goes to the thoughts. Because of this interest or belief in thoughts, we overlook the present and clear nature within us.

༄

Your nature is the knowing space containing all appearances. What is the nature of that presence? It obviously exists, for you are present. It is also aware, for you know all that appears and disappears. Your true nature has no problems, worries or suffering, so it is peace or happiness itself. Recognize the immediate and wordless presence of your true nature in direct, non-conceptual knowing. With this seeing, it is evident that the limited person you have taken yourself to be has never existed, except as an assumption. When this is understood, suffering, doubt, seeking and personal problems vanish entirely.

Your true nature is not an object. That is why it is sometimes referred to as emptiness or 'no thing'. But that emptiness is not a void or absence. It is brightly cognizant and aware. It is the space in which everything else comes and goes. It is there even in deep sleep, for if dreams or other experiences appear, they are immediately cognized—where?—in awareness. Even samadhi or other 'formless states' are registered in awareness. Otherwise, how could we know them or speak of them afterwards?

When the mind is not fixated on conceptual images of who and what we are, the state of being present and aware is suffused with a natural peace and a complete absence of suffering. It is not a neutral, blank state at all. We overlook it for a time because we are habituated to looking for gross sensations of bodily pleasure or mental stimulation. The real peace and joy is that 'peace that passes all understanding', meaning it is not graspable by the mind. The Hindu sages pointed to our true nature using the terms being, awareness and happiness. See the truth of who you are and this becomes immediately clear.

There is no awakened teacher, no teaching, no dharma, no transmission. There is no seeker, no bondage, no conditioning, no practice, no meditation, no path, no goal, no attainment, no stabilizing, no deepening, no embodying, no transformation, no purification, no growth, no development, no awakening, no realization, no liberation. There is nothing to obtain from books, retreats or satsangs. There is nothing to gain by meditation, stillness, silence, renunciation, loving kindness, selfless service or good works. There is no intrinsic value in visions, mystical experiences, supernatural powers, manifesting abundance, receiving divine favors, initiations and the like. There is no karma, no sin, no merit, no virtue, no destiny, no duty. There is no past, no present, no future, no time, no space, no causality, no world, no body, no mind, no soul, no individual, no person, no you, no I. None of these things have the slightest reality or substance whatsoever. They are purely conceptual, mere appearances in imagination. Imagination itself is completely insubstantial! Look within—there is only presence-awareness. Look without—there is only the same presence-awareness. It is unchanging, undivided, whole, sufficient, full, complete, ever-fresh and ever-present. You are that and nothing but that.

Your true nature is completely clear and present right now. When you say 'I know I am' it is not a theory. You can say this with total conviction because your own presence is self-evident. It is so evident that we overlook the implication of it. The essence of all teachings is: 'know yourself'. Your self is already present and known. Otherwise, how can you say 'I know I am'? All descriptions of reality are only about this true nature that is present right now.

The 'I' who is aware is presence-awareness. That does not disappear. The belief in the separate 'I' or entity standing apart from awareness is only an assumption, a concept. The appearance or disappearance of that concept makes no difference to awareness. There never has been a separate 'I'. It is only assumed to exist. Seeing through that notion, that is, seeing it as false, snaps the belief in its reality. There is no basic change. But all the ideas and identifications based on that belief are no longer believed. Hence the personal doubts and suffering are resolved.

*Addendum*

# Clarifying One's Essential Identity
## ~ an Interview with John Wheeler

*Question: I have been studying Dzogchen for the past fifteen years or so. In your book you say that you spent enough time with "Sailor" Bob Adamson such that he was able to bring it all to a direct stop.*

John: Yes, you could say that.

*Q: I have prepared a few questions. Some of them have been answered since reading your book "Shining in Plain View." In reading your book it came together more solidly for once. I became really suspicious about the thoughts. My sense is that as long as there is a sense of a perceiver—and until the perceiver dissolves—one is still going to conclude that the false "I" is real. You say that you have to come to a direct realization that the "I" does not exist. That really resonates. But you say that there is a sense of being, a sense of watching. I have all of that happening also, but I tend to call all of that the "I."*

John: Hmmm.

*Q: I wonder how much of my confusion is due to semantics based on different traditions.*

John: I was acquainted with various non-duality teachings for fifteen or twenty years, primarily through reading and meeting a few Western teachers. When I met "Sailor" Bob I met somebody who had a living teacher, Nisargadatta Maharaj. Nisargadatta was a highly regarded and acclaimed teacher in the Navnath Sampradaya tradition in Western India. That tradition traces its roots back through nine main teachers to about the 11th century and then all the way back to the mythical guru Dattatreya. Anyway, after a period of years of searching and trying various spiritual approaches, "Sailor" Bob got his questions answered when he met Nisargadatta Maharaj.

For me, meeting "Sailor" Bob was very different from my previous experiences. Sitting down and talking with him really clarified things for me. As a result, I am a firm believer of the importance of such contact. All the traditions say that the essential understanding is not conceptual. It is not mental. It is not an object to be grasped. It is not something that the mind works out. When we read about these pointers in books, it almost invariably gets reformulated back into a concept and turned into something objective. As a result, we tend to miss the essential point. So what Bob's teacher did for him, and what Bob did for me, was to point out the basics, keeping things very simple, direct and clear. And, of course, this was done in the context of his own direct experience of what he was talking about. This is what I try to do through sharing this also.

Now in Tibetan Buddhism, as far as I am aware, they are always talking about something called intrinsic awareness. That, in my view, is the "whole enchilada," so to speak. It is the core. In Advaita Vedanta, they have a very similar thing. They refer to it as consciousness or awareness. It gets discussed with its own set of terms. So in trying to appreciate these teachings, the most important thing is to clarify precisely what they are talking about. What are they pointing out for us to understand? These traditions often say that to recognize our nature as this essential awareness is synonymous with freedom. And, conversely, not to be aware of this is the definition of a suffering being under the sway of ignorance. You have been acquainted with these teachings for many years now. Is this part of it clear? Do you understand what is being pointed to by the words awareness, consciousness and so forth?

Q: *Yes, what you say is clear. The only difference for me is that when awareness is viewed through the lens of the ego, it becomes consciousness.*

John: You could say that. That is very similar to a distinction that Nisargadatta often made. In his dialogues he makes a distinction between consciousness and awareness.

Q: *Yes. There is a big difference.*

John: Well, it is all words. It depends on what you mean by those. Consciousness, as Nisargadatta uses the term, is a material product that arises when the body is conceived and subsequently dissolves at death. This consciousness (or what we might loosely call "mind") allows us to conceive thoughts and generate the sense "I am" as a thought or experience. This "I am" sense is dependent on the consciousness/mind, which in turn is dependent on the body. So even the "I am" sense is impermanent. But as Nisargadatta goes on to say, you are still present as that pure awareness that is knowing the arising and setting of that (relative) consciousness. He sometimes asked, "What were you eight days prior to conception?" The questioner might say, "I don't know." The reason for this is that the body and the consciousness were not present. There was no instrument to register anything or say anything. Nisargadatta would say, "That in you to which that thought 'I don't know' arises was there. That is what you are." He sometimes referred to that as pure awareness or pure being. Since it is not an object, it cannot be known objectively. However, it is self-knowing or self-cognizing. You cannot know it as an object, but neither can you deny it because its presence is self-evident. It is the undeniable presence registering even the sense "I am." You could say it is the pure, wordless presence beyond the sense of "I am."

*Q: One other thing! Clarity is defined very specifically in Dzogchen as "no perceiver." It is also said that awareness is aware of itself.*

John: OK.

*Q: However, first consciousness enters rigpa (intrinsic awareness). When consciousness turns into rigpa, the belief in self falls apart. But the perceiver dissolves into vast open expanse, as described by Longchenpa (the thirteenth century Dzogchen master). Then you are simply being in this moment, which is ineffable, undefinable, totally radiant, expansive, luminous—all those things. And there is no sense of a "me." Longchenpa says, "Rest without reifying an external object, without reifying an internal self." We are not turning this [pointing to the glass on the table] into a "glass" by defining it conceptually, and we are not turning this [pointing to the heart] into a "perceiver." These are things that feel intrinsically true about the whole process. However, at this point there is still "me" trying to see it! When I read your book, there was a moment when this conceptualizing all stopped. But then it came back in again.*

John: I will just talk about it in my terms. It will be much simpler than the traditional approach. You can approach this from the perspective of philosophical speculation and make a lot of subtle distinctions about things. It is an attempt to articulate what is happening at a very, very subtle level of experience and language. That is all fine. I enjoy that stuff myself to a certain extent. But in terms of getting to the essential point of recognizing who we are and stepping free of suffering, it is actually quite a bit simpler. So let me try to present it as I present it.

Q: OK.

John: All the teachings of non-duality are basically pointing to the presence of something in us to be recognized as our essential nature. So the question—and real point of it all—is: what is this essential nature? The interesting point here is that we are not looking for something that is not present. We are not looking for something in the future. We are not looking for something that is a different state or experience. Not at all. We are starting from the perspective that our true intrinsic nature is already present and always has been. It must be fully present now. To have a clear recognition of this is the heart of everything.

Conversely, to be unclear about our true nature, to be mistaken about what this is and to misconceive who we are is the basic ignorance or misunderstanding. This non-recognition becomes the cause of the subsequent misunderstandings, attachments and confusions. So, I often talk about two aspects. One is pointing out the positive truth of who you are. The other is dissolving the mistaken idea of what you wrongly take yourself to be. These are really the same thing. It is just saying it in two different ways. As Nisargadatta once said, you can push the cart or pull the cart. It does not matter as long as you keep it rolling! As you relinquish the mistaken belief of who you are, what is left remaining is your real nature. On the other hand, if you clarify the truth of who you are, then that understanding dissolves the mistaken ideas. It is just a matter of clarifying one's essential identity. That is how I view it.

Our true nature is often pointed out as intrinsic or innate awareness. The question is—do we recognize that? Do we see it for ourselves? Do we know ourselves to be that? Let us bring this into the present moment and make this simpler. Right here, right now, as we sit here tonight, can we recognize and acknowledge our essential being and its nature of awareness? Is it emphatically clear, without any doubt at all? If this is unclear, then we are going to misperceive who or what we are. And there will arise a mistaken view of ourselves. We will grasp onto something else—a mistaken sense of "I."

Right now, in our direct experience, this intrinsic nature must be present. Can we recognize it? Do we know it clearly? It must be here because we are here, our being is present. The way this got pointed out to me was as follows. "Sailor" Bob Adamson had me pause and recognize a couple of things. One was what he called presence, or the sense of being, this simple sense of "I am," the recognition that you are. He asked me, "Can you sense or do you know that you are present? Is there a sense of being?" Of course, this is undeniable! And he pointed out this sense of awareness by asking, "Are you aware? Are you aware right now of thoughts, feelings and perceptions happening?" This was something that I could recognize. I think that anybody can. Basically, we know as clear as day that we are here and there is awareness present. So the way he introduced this was to point out this undeniable sense of presence-awareness and get us to look at that.

This is really the essence of it. This is what it gets to—to recognize this presence of awareness that is with us right now. This is important because we are often under the impression that this is something very subtle. We imagine that it is hard to see or that something extraordinary has to happen before it will be revealed. What is very interesting about this approach is how simple it is. The presence of awareness is really what these traditions are pointing to as our identity. It is already here. It is very simply evident and known. When you pause and reflect on the fact that you are, you notice that this sense of being is not inert. It is quite vivid. It is quite aware. So this aware presence or presence-awareness, or whatever you want to call it, is crystal clear and completely available. It is very, very simple. The fact that we have not recognized it is where the mistaken identity or false sense of "me" comes from. The point I am making is that, as we sit here, what we truly are is this bare or simple sense of being present and aware. It is nothing more than that.

Now another way to approach this is through discarding all things that I am not. For example, right now we can see thoughts coming up and passing away. We can observe feelings coming up and passing away. It is the same with sensations and perceptions. These different objects just come and go. They are transitory. They do not remain with us for any length of time. So they are not going to be the essence of who we are. If you set those aside and you look to see what is here apart from those things, you find that there is still something present. You still are, and you know that you are. Your presence continues, in spite of the changing appearances. As the thoughts come in and out, there is an awareness of them. When they are there you are aware of them. When they disappear, you are quite aware that they are not there. So that presence of awareness still remains.

The key to recognizing our true nature is to realize that it is one hundred percent absolutely present. The truth is that we can actually recognize it quite easily. The thing that tends to happen is that we have a hard time believing that it is this simple. We think, "This cannot be who we are. This is so obvious. This is too simple. This cannot possibly be what they are talking about."

Things drastically changed for me through the confirmation from "Sailor" Bob, based on his experience with his teacher and his own lived understanding, that it is that simple. When we pause and recognize the pure sense of being and awareness, this is the direct, absolute, clear, recognition of our intrinsic true nature. This is not a partial, momentary, vague recognition. We are coming face to face with what the non-dual traditions have been pointing out all along. It is very rare that we would ever hear about this or get this pointed out, much less spend any time probing into the meaning of it. Because of the way that we have been conditioned to view things, we typically think "I am this. I am that. I am a body. I am a thought. I am a person. I have certain attributes." But all of those things are concepts. This immediate awareness that we actually are is not a concept at all. It is not in the mind. You start to see the difference between the idea of what we think ourselves to be and the non-conceptual presence of who we truly are.

The non-dual teachings have been saying all along that we are not in the mind, we are not an image, we are not a construction in thought, we are not something objective. As you start to lock in on that, you start to realize that this is what it has always been about. All of the traditions are basically saying that our true nature is what is real. To recognize this is the whole essence of it. Then one's view radically changes. It certainly changed for me when I realized that we are not looking for anything that is distant, complicated or hard to understand. Once you get a basic sense of this, you discover some very incredible things about this basic aware presence. There is nothing mundane about it at all.

So recognize for yourself your true nature as that undeniable sense of being, which is both present and aware. Notice that as various thoughts, feelings and perceptions arise and pass your presence does not change. Does this sense of being alter in the slightest? Does it go anywhere? Does it have any variation? Does it come or go? Do you lose it? Understand that in this looking, we are not bringing anything new into the picture at all. We could have looked at this years ago, but we just simply never considered it!

It is important that this recognition of our essential nature is very clear and solid. If this is not clear, the mind will constantly jump back into the conceptualization process, with all of the doubts and questions. This is because the mind is searching to know what is true about ourselves. If the truth of who we are is not clear, it leaves the mind trying to answer those questions by going back into the only place it is familiar with—which is the conceptual process. So it is essential to recognize what we are and allow that to become very, very clear. We have seen our true nature to be that sense of being-awareness. It is already here. It is easily recognized. It is constantly with us and unchanged by appearances.

Q: *In deep sleep, I do not have that sense.*

John: I suggest becoming familiar with this presently in the waking state. Then the issue of deep sleep will take care of itself. But often what happens is that before we allow ourselves to get familiar with what is being pointed out, we stop the looking by jumping to these edge cases and getting sidetracked in speculation. There is a lot you can see right now. We have only touched the tip of the iceberg! Let's continue to look into our present true nature. It seems simple but is actually very profound. There is a lot of depth to it.

Do you need to wait for the future to recognize what you are? How many of us have been waiting for something to happen in the future, assuming that somehow the answer lies there? When you realize that this is about your present nature, then you see you do not have to wait for the future. You set aside that concept.

Does this recognition involve a path, a practice, a technique or process?

Q: *No.*

John: It is important to see that. Is there any effort at all involved in being what you are?

Q: *Only if you are in a state of fear or suffering.*

John: Well, I am asking you right now! Are you making any effort to recognize that you are?

Q: *Well, no. But I brought that up because that is one of my main issues.*

John: Yet you find that in your direct experience, natural awareness is already present. It is naturally and effortlessly present. It is not a maintenance state. It is not something that you manufacture. It is not something you have to get to or achieve. We often make those assumptions. But when you look in present experience, the assumptions are not valid.

Let us continue with a bit more investigation. Is this innate awareness an object that you see as something apart from yourself? In other words, in recognizing presence-awareness is it something over there, while you are here? Do you say, "There it is, and here I am"? Is that what you actually see in your experience? Is this innate presence of awareness anything objective at all? Look for yourself. We know it is here. We know we are. We know we are aware. In the recognition of this, is it something that stands apart with characteristics that you can grasp objectively? Is your being a thing? Is it a thought? Is it a particular perception?

Q: *I do not experience it as a totality yet. I experience everything in it. But what appears seems to be separate. So I am stuck right there.*

John: Let's not lose the thread of what we are seeing here. We are seeing the fact that, as far as we can tell, presence, which means the sense of being-awareness, is not a thought, experience or object that you grasp hold of. It is not an object and yet, it is undeniably, irrefutably present. It is a very interesting thing, really.

There are a couple more points to consider to drive home the basic recognition of things. Is it that you are one thing and awareness is another thing? Or is it that you are that which is present and aware? Can you make any distinction between awareness and your own presence? We already saw that awareness is not an object. What this really means is that there is actually no separation between our own nature and that which is aware. This point has profound implications, immense implications. The non-dual teachings are saying the nature of reality is this ineffable awareness-presence. And in our immediate experience we discover that this awareness is our identity. It is what we are. We cannot find a separation between ourselves and awareness. It is not that there is you and there is awareness. You find that you ARE that which is aware. You are presence-awareness itself.

Finally, there is one other aspect to mention. The body feels experiences, or the mind has various thoughts and feelings. So naturally the mind might have questions, problems or worries. Those are clearly something that is occurring in the mind. They are thoughts. Or the body might be feeling a pain or some other sensation. But does the presence of awareness actually have those things? Is the awareness itself subject or victim to those appearances? If we grant that psychological suffering is a product of or an appearance in the mind, can we say that the actual awareness itself has any suffering or problems? If you grant that is only the mind that has thoughts and feelings, you can start to recognize something quite interesting. Awareness, which we have seen is what we actually are, has no suffering. It is not limited by it. It is not subject to the states of the body and mind. That leads us to the recognition that intrinsic, innate presence is completely free of any limitation or suffering at all.

Let us review what we have covered so far. We see that that our nature is the simple sense of presence-awareness. It is here, effortlessly recognized. It is not in the future. It is not something we need to produce or maintain. It is not a practice. It is not something objective that we can grasp a hold of. Yet it is utterly undeniable. We can find no separation between ourselves and what is present and aware. Essentially, we are that. While the body and mind experience various states and conditions, awareness itself is innately free. Because this awareness is not objective, it is not in the flow of time. We cannot say it begins, changes or ends. How can something that is not an object be subject to time or change?

You begin to realize an incredible possibility that has always been totally present but just overlooked. There is nothing being pointed out that is foreign or difficult to comprehend. It is so innate and present that there is no need to even bring in concepts such as enlightenment, awakening, liberation or any such thing. Those are too crude, too objective. When those concepts are emphasized, people start to think, "When awakening happens, then I will be there. Then I will see this. Then I will know what this is about." It turns out that to know who you are, you do not need any of that at all. They are useless concepts. They keep people looking away from the simplicity—and profundity—of things. If we were not precisely clear what some of these great traditions were pointing to as our true nature, it is very, very important to hear this and recognize this for yourself.

Now what I find, though, is that many of us have heard stuff like this for a long time. We may have heard about it through books or popular teachers. It was not foreign to me, and I am sure it is not foreign to you either. But the change that occurred for me through my contact with "Sailor" Bob was the vivid recognition of how close, near and available this is. That was not clear to me till then. What I missed was the fact that what is being pointed to is already present in my experience. All the teachers I had met up till then lacked a clear understanding of things because they were overtly or subtly implying that full recognition of who we are is not immediately present. They were not able to point that out. However, that can and will get pointed out directly by someone with a clear and direct understanding. This is what the teachers coming from the non-dual traditions have confirmed from their experience. And you will find that there is nothing beyond this.

At one point, I viewed myself as a seeker who was basically on the hunt for enlightenment, the great future attainment. It got pointed out very quickly that this was all just a concept, that I was looking in the wrong direction. While we are pursuing the state of enlightenment, we are overlooking the fact that everything that is being pointed to is actually already here. In seeing this, we can let that concept go. We can appreciate and relax with an acknowledgement of this already present fact of what we are. "Sailor" Bob was suggesting that we start from the position or the recognition that we already are that. You already know that. It is already attained. Why not begin with this as your baseline, instead of saying, "Where is it? How am I going to get there? I cannot see it. I need to get enlightened." For most people, this is a radical change of perspective.

Looking in this way allows you to dismantle many other unnecessary concepts. For example, a common notion is that it is a matter of relaxing into our true nature over and over again. We think that somehow this will enable us to get more and more stabilized or closer to it. But even that is a conceptual overlay. It is not necessary

*Q: It is still a perceiver.*

John: Yes. We have already seen that it is not that there is you as a separate entity and another thing called presence-awareness. It is nothing like that. We saw that this is what you are. So if you are this awareness and you cannot find a separation, then the notion that I am going to relax into it is purely conceptual. If it is what you are, how can you get out of it? It is totally effortless to be what you already are. Who is going to relax into it? These beliefs and assumptions begin to stand out as conceptual constructs. So talking about relaxing into presence implies that we are not this. But we are this. We should recognize the truth of what we already are.

Once you get this basic thing pointed out, that what we have been seeking is what we already are, you see that there is nothing you are going to do to achieve that or enhance it. Where can you go from there? That is the whole ball game. It is like searching for the North Pole. Once you arrive there, where can you go? Any way you move, you start heading south again. So, full stop! Seeing your actual position, you are not going to move anywhere because that will not get you any closer. Anywhere you try to move is going to be a fall away from that.

From this recognition, you start to realize that what has been hanging us up are the concepts, the mistaken beliefs about who we are. Let us say that I still believe the notion that the goal is distant from me and I need to do something to get there. That is a belief. Based on that, I will assume that I am a separate being, that the true nature is apart from me and that I am progressing towards it. So that "I" thought, which is the notion that I stand as something apart from the intrinsic reality, becomes a solid belief. It gets taken as real. However, the whole conceptual framework is just an appearance of thought arising and setting right in this present awareness. That awareness is already at the goal, and you already are that.

So the whole conceptual framework is misconceived. Yet it will cause suffering. Instead realizing the already present freedom, the mind conceives of a separation. We believe that we are something separate. The sense of limitation comes in and the mind begins to construct a framework of how it is going to achieve oneness. But it is invalid because you are not separate. As these concepts get pointed out, they can be seen and discarded. A weight falls off. Every time you bring up one of these conceptual frameworks, you spot it and the belief drops out of it. The suffering and the bondage wrapped up into that falls off your shoulders.

It is important to understand where the concepts come from, what they are rooted in, and how that mechanism works. Once you see that the concept of a separate self and all the notions that go with it are not valid, you no longer believe them. In not grasping hold of them, where does it leave you? It leaves you naturally and effortlessly in the true nature that you are with no suffering due to belief in false concepts. You are not really gaining anything, but you are simply discarding the concepts that were generating unnecessary, conceptually-based suffering.

In my experience of this, what happened was that the true nature was pointed out and recognized very clearly. But then my doubts, fears and beliefs from the past would arise in the middle of this clear knowing of my identity as awareness. This was distracting and triggered suffering. But then I started to see what was happening. Erroneous concepts based on the view of a limited self, which the mind had picked up from in the past, were appearing, and the energy of belief was going into them. I was assuming those thoughts to be valid statements of myself and taking them seriously. The clear and simple truth of who I am was being overlooked. It was nothing more complicated than this, but in all the years of seeking I had missed this basic point.

The vast majority of seekers out there are not clear on the basic recognition of their true nature. They simply are not. And this even applies to those interested in Buddhism, Zen, Dzogchen, Advaita Vedanta or other modern derivatives of these traditions.

*Q: The essential teachings are seldom ever given, even in the Dzogchen community. So most practitioners lack a basic recognition.*

John: In my view there are not that many people out there that talking about this in a direct way without mixing in unnecessary concepts. "Sailor" Bob does it. Perhaps there are a few others. The basic points are embedded in the traditions obviously, but when you go out in the current spiritual marketplace, you rarely see this presented clearly.

It is very, very important to have a direct pointing out of your true nature. It is often best to have this pointed out in a face-to-face, live conversation, so that you can hear it, resonate with it, ask questions, and allow it to sink in as your direct experience. It is hard, if not impossible, to read about what I am talking about and make much sense out of it. It is entirely non-conceptual. So if you read a book about presence-awareness, you can come away thinking, "That is an interesting idea. That sounds really incredible. I wish I understood it." But when the basic point of this clicks in your direct experience and you have a taste of that for yourself, it is a significant turning point. You then know that what is being pointed to is not in books. It is not something special that teachers have. It is not something distant at all. You know that wherever you go, that all that was ever being pointed to is shining in your direct experience as the undeniable sense of being-awareness that is already here. That is what they were always talking about. Now you know! This became clear to me after talking with "Sailor" Bob. Suddenly, the point of it all dawned. After all those years, I knew what they were talking about. It became clear to me what this actually is.

I saw that my doubts, fears, worries and problems would erupt into this recognition of who I am. I did not yet know what was going on. So my sense of suffering was still active. I talked about this with "Sailor" Bob for two or three days. I would be feeling really clear, with a sense that "this is so obvious." Then something would come up in my mind about work or health. I would get wrapped up in a personal issue or some spiritual concept. Suddenly I would be back into the suffering. That was puzzling for me. Fortunately, I was able to go back and talk about this stuff and get it resolved.

Just as you understand the truth of what you are, you can also understand suffering. You can understand what it is, where it comes from and how it can be resolved. I know very, very few people out there who are clear on this aspect. You meet a lot of people who will tell you, "I know who I am. I am awakened. I know I am consciousness. I am awareness." And then they say, "But the conditioning and the suffering keeps coming up." If you ask them what they are going to do about it, they do not have a real answer! They do not know where suffering comes from. They do not know why it arises. We think, "I hope someday its going to work itself out then I will be free." But that is not really an answer at all. I started to see this in the contemporary spiritual scene. People I had known who had been at it for years and years were still subject to doubts and suffering, even after going to countless satsangs, retreats and so-called "awakened" teachers.

The real answer comes through a clear understanding. Passively waiting for suffering to depart is not sufficient in my view. When I talk about suffering, I refer to the emotional turbulence, doubts, worries, fears, concerns about myself, what people think of me, the feeling of being a separate individual, whatever you can think of that is contrary to this innate sense of peace. I am not referring to bodily pain. That is part of the natural organic intelligence of things. So what we are really dealing with is how to understand and resolve the psychological suffering that is generated by false concepts of who we are. Then you are not going to be a victim of doubts, suffering and worries. You are not going to feel like you are a separate seeker. You are not going to feel that other people know things that you do not know. You are not going to feel that you are missing something. You are not going to be engulfed in black, dark moods any longer. All these kinds of things come from causes which can be addressed. They come from a mistaken view of ourselves, and they can be resolved.

This is done in conjunction with the recognition of the truth of who you are. As that recognition comes to the forefront, it contradicts or eliminates the root cause, that basic mistaken identity. This is completely workable. It absolutely, emphatically gets to the root of it once and for all. Those who say suffering is inevitable or an inherent part of the nature of things are entirely mistaken.

*Q: I have been dealing with some physical pain issues.*

John: I have dealt with that myself, too.

*Q: It appears for you that there is no longer any doubt that there is no separate "I." Is that true?*

John: Yes.

*Q: Then when physical pain arises in a real level of intensity, does the awareness stay for you?*

John: Definitely, yes. And the reason is very simple. The pain is arising and registered in the awareness, so the awareness does not go anywhere. We already determined that perceptions, feelings and thoughts going through do not disturb, contradict or eliminate the basic presence of awareness. We may not recognize that or note that at some stage because all of our focus and emotional energy goes so much onto the experience. But it does not mean that the being or the awareness literally goes anywhere. The fact of it is that you cannot have those experiences without awareness. They are still occurring as experiences in awareness, aren't they?

*Q: But take the case of someone like Ramana Maharshi. He had* cancer in the upper arm which basically ate him until he died. He acknowledged there was great pain, but he also acknowledged that there was no doubt, that the awareness was not affected at all. Right?

John: It was the same with Nisargadatta, "Sailor" Bob's teacher. He died of a throat cancer that took his life after about three years. He kept teaching and talking right to the very last day. He could hardly talk, and he was still communicating this message right until the last moments of his life. So somehow he was able to go through these experiences.

Q: *It appears that he was able to sit there as awareness and simply let things arise in spite of the physical experiences, right?*

John: That appeared to be the case.

Q: *And it was the same with Ramana Maharshi, right?*

John: And it will be the same for you, too! Because the truth of it is that when things come up, whatever they happen to be, you will still be there as that awareness. This we have already seen.

Q: *For me right now the pain seems to drive me to such distraction that I stop knowing my nature as awareness.*

John: Apparently! But do not bring back in the notion that your nature is something to be perceived as an object that you can gain and lose. You are not a separate entity apart from that awareness and you never will be. So the whole notion that you cannot get back to the awareness or you cannot see it is based on a false assumption. It does not matter what you think. You are that awareness. You will always be that. There is nothing you can do to get away from it. It is not a matter of relaxing into it, focusing on it or obtaining it. That is all conceptual. It is much more basic than that. It is what you are innately and always will be.

So when you really start to get that point, you realize that the idea that you have to get to your true nature is fallacious. The notion that you have to focus, hold your mind in a certain way or pay attention, has nothing to do with this. It is much more basic. All the thoughts, distractions, efforts or any other experiences always appear in this ever-present awareness, which is naturally present with no effort.

*Q: Awareness, if free, is free to not even look at the pain. Is this so?*

John: Well, there is no need for that. Who we are is not really subject or victim to those experiences. There is no need to maneuver away from it, to embrace it, push it away or anything of the sort. Typically, when we are experiencing pain we think, "This should not be happening to me. I would like to get away from this. This isn't right." That kind of relationship with what is appearing starts to fall away. If you are having pain in the body, you are probably going to do something to address it. That is fine at a relative level. But when you look a bit more deeply, you see that there is simply awareness in which things are happening, even a pain in my leg or whatever. The awareness is one thing, the pain is something else. It is an experience.

The other layer that gets in there that confuses things is the conceptual process, the mind's interpretation of what is going on. It adds unnecessary conceptualizing onto the experience. For example, you think, "I am here feeling pain. This is happening to me. This is not good. It should not be happening. I wish this would stop." All of that is simply being spun up in the thought process. The awareness does not have those opinions. It is just registering what is. And the pain is just happening. It is an impersonal happening. So this layer of conceptualization is where the problem creeps in. Why? Because your nature of awareness is already free and has no problems. The thoughts, feeling and perceptions that come up are just transitory things that move through this awareness. They do not have any opinion about whether they should be there or not. They are just happening, just doing their thing. So where is the problem? So why introduce a third entity into the equation? Why not be with what is and not identify it as some experience for a self which is not even there! If you do not interpret something through that reference point, then there is not a conceptual position. Everything may appear just like it always has from an outside viewpoint. But with an understanding of the conceptual nature of suffering, the suffering is no longer taken as real. There is no need to introduce that third component in there.

*Q: So in your own case I understand that you have had some physical health issues.*

John: Yes.

*Q: So in that situation, worry does not come up and get you spinning? You do not buy it when it comes up?*

John: Mostly it does not come up because I have seen through that. You can see that too. Once you understand that all this suffering, worry and turbulence is being generated at a conceptual level in the mind based on a misunderstanding and that what it is based on is not real, you are done with it. It is all thought based. It depends on giving those beliefs and concepts reality. For example, here is an exaggerated case so you can get a feel for this. If I suddenly realize that this body is deathly ill and is on its way out, and I am told by doctors, "We do not know if you are going to make it or not." There are a couple of ways of responding to this. The objective fact is that the body is just a mortal creature. It was born and it will eventually pass. This is an objective fact. And the awareness simply registers what appears. It could be a healthy body, a sick body, a young body, an old body or a dying body. From the perspective of awareness it does not have any preference. It does not have a value judgment. It does not say, "Oh, when I look out this should be a young person or a healthy person. It just registers whatever is there. And until there is conceptualization, there is no suffering in any of that. However, imagine I were to say, "I am dying. I am sick. This is happening to me." Then this would start to bring in this sense of self, the notion that my being or my identity is getting wrapped up with the events.

This would be mistaking the true awareness that I am with this conceptualizing process, which we have already decided is not who I am. The mind is creating a confusion by melding together the sense of our true nature and this conceptual identity. Then you come out with the statement, "Here I am. I am dying." And suffering arises with that belief. The mind goes into a panic. There is the notion that my being or my identity is ending or that something traumatic is happening to me. The truth is that this is completely erroneous.

This is where you start to see where suffering comes in. Suffering is not given, and it is not natural. It is not part of what is really present, in fact. It is a very specifically constructed mental framework based on an erroneous view of things. So if the mind constructs the notion "I am dying" and believes it, then a certain amount of energy goes into that belief. That is when I start to have psychological suffering. Then the mind will jump to additional concepts, such as "What do I do now? This should not be happening. I have got to change this. Oh my God, I do not want to die. There are so many things I want to do." At that point you are in a whole cloud of concepts and taking it as quite real. But it is all thought based. It is all springing from the mistaken identification. So this starts to show where suffering comes in.

You start to realize that suffering, as I am defining it, is a creation of the thought process. So "Sailor" Bob makes the comment, "What's wrong if you are not thinking about it?" It is a way he sums up this whole thing. From this, you start to see some interesting things. For example, a question is a thought. A worry is a thought. A sense of a problem is a thought. Concern about what others are thinking about me is a thought. Worry about what I should do is a thought. Your beliefs and sense of who you are is a collection of thoughts. You suddenly realize that all of these things are created by the conceptual mind. If someone were to come in and wipe all of those thoughts aside, what would be left? Only presence-awareness and possibly some feelings and perceptions passing through, but no personal suffering or conceptualization based on the separate "me" idea. So—aha! The resolution presents itself.

*Q: In this case there is just awareness and physical pain. You might not define it as physical pain?*

John: Yes, you might not even do that. Even labeling it as physical pain is actually a thought construct. You may find that the actual physical pain is not quite as intense as the mind makes it up to be. You can see this for example in the case of an injury or accident. For the most part, the body usually deals with it. If the mind jumps on it and really starts amplifying it, building it up and expanding it, then the psychological trouble is often more traumatic than the physical situation.

What we are getting to here is the understanding of where suffering comes from. To see that suffering is a creation of thought is very important because if you are going to get to the cause, you have to understand how it works. A lot of people think that suffering is based on external events. But they are entirely misperceiving where it is coming from. So how can they ever really get to the root of it?

So suffering is a product of thought for the most part. When you look closely at those thoughts, you notice that the ones that really grab us are the ones that are talking about our sense of self or personal identity. If I am sitting here and I am thinking any random thought, such as "The moon is shining tonight." Well, for most of us, so what? There is not much of a reaction. It is just a passing thought. But if a thought comes in that says, "I am no good" or "Somebody does not like me" or "I am going to die" or whatever it might be, then things get stickier. What is actually happening when such thoughts come up is that they start to define me. They say something about me and who I am. Looking in this way gives us a more accurate view of what this suffering really is. "Sailor" Bob pointed this out to me once. He defined suffering as self-centered thinking. In other words, the thoughts concerning my identity or sense of "me" are the ones that really get us stuck.

If you tell me you think there is something wrong with you, there is not much of a reaction here. But if I think there is something wrong with me, then …. "Wait, wait, wait a minute!" (laughing). I do not like that at all! Why don't I like that? Because it is an incorrect statement of who I truly am. So when you trace the suffering down to the next level, you see these thoughts are about the self. If you are observant, you start to see a pattern to all of this. It is not that there is just "a" pain in the body. Rather, it is that "I" am in pain, or "I" have got this pain, or "I" do not like this pain. So these thoughts get referenced to a sense of self, an idea of self. You realize it is not just the thoughts that are the problem. It is the way that they reference the sense of "I." This root notion of "I" is described in different ways, either as the ego sense, the separate self, the "I"-thought or the separate person. However you wish to describe it, it is the core of this whole mechanism. It is what all the self-centered concepts seem to be referring to.

All of the identifications attach to this core belief. The reason they are troublesome is because that core belief is taken as valid, when in fact it is completely erroneous.

If you tell me, "John, you are a blue elephant." I would not believe that for a second. I would not take that seriously. I do not associate that concept as who I am. That notion is very patently false. I do not believe it or identify with it at all. And, as a consequence, it does not trouble me in the least. A concept only troubles you when you take it on board and believe it. Without believing it, it is powerless. So in order to believe and suffer under a concept, such as "I am not enlightened," you must have the intermediate step of taking the "I"-thought as valid. You have to have the "I" that is not enlightened or whatever the identification happens to be. This understanding allows us to get to the roots of this very directly. Instead of picking off all the possible thoughts and beliefs that we have picked up over the years, we can take this to the core and realize that there is a lynch pin holding all of this together. If you knock out the root cause, the belief in the "I," then there is nowhere for any other identifications to take hold. Nothing attaches anymore. This shows that it is possible to expose the core of the belief and resolve the whole network of suffering conclusively.

It is important to see where all the concepts and beliefs came from. It is all just stuff that we picked up over the years because we did not know any better. The notion of being a limited, separate "I" gets picked up in the mind at a young age. It is not questioned. It is assumed to be real. From there, we start believing in a lot of things that are attached to the sense of self. People tell us a lot of things. "You are a body. You are a good boy. You are a student. You are this, that and the other." All these things are basically just conceptual definitions, right? When we become spiritual seekers we start identifying with a lot of spiritual beliefs, such as "I am a spiritual person. I am a Buddhist. I am on the path to enlightenment." But the truth is that you are not on a path at all. That is a total construct. It is all still definitions of a seemingly separate entity. Only now you have a new set of definitions. You are a seeker after enlightenment. Those notions generate just as much suffering as experienced by any so-called non-spiritual person. At the core of it is the notion that I am not whole and complete. I am separate. There is something apart from me. I am not there yet. I am not good enough. Hopefully something is going to fix me. You are still completely locked into this conceptual framework. Spiritual seekers may or may not be ready to question some of these spiritual concepts. But they are still part of the same mechanism. Your nature of innate awareness is not a Buddhist or a Dzogchen practitioner!

So how do you take care of this whole thing and wrap up the show? The central proposition is that the reason we suffer is due to a residual belief in the reality of this core concept. That belief fuels the rest of these habitual thoughts and keeps us focused on the mind. We assume that the central "I" is valid. I had heard about this as a concept for many years before meeting "Sailor" Bob. I remember reading some Buddhist teachings that described the root of all suffering was the belief in a sense of separate self. I suppose every good Buddhist knows that! But what I did not realize was how to apply that and what it really meant. Even though I had been exposed to that pointer years ago, I was clearly still functioning from a sense that I was a separate self.

For example, when I went to Australia to see "Sailor" Bob, I was thinking, "I am going to Australia. I need to get answers. I need to find enlightenment. Perhaps he can help me. I am going to get something that I a missing." It was not clear to me that this whole mindset was a complete belief system centered upon a seemingly separate self. As that intrinsic presence of awareness which we truly are, I did not have any need to go to Australia! I did not need to get anything. There was nothing he could give me, in an absolute sense. I even recall e-mailing him at one point about the desire to see him and he said there was no need to come! He pointed out that I had everything I needed already. But I was still operating under the false belief in the separate "I." And it turns out that there was something that he helped me with, which was simply to show me what was happening and to expose the false belief in who I thought I was so that it could fall away in that seeing. Even though I got nothing from "Sailor" Bob, I will be forever grateful for that nothing!

So the "I" thought is a total illusion. It is not even there. It is a complete assumption. There is no evidence that it even exists. It is a concept that has no real existence at all, except as an assumption. When you really have a good look, you discover that the separate person that we have taken ourself to be is an illusion. To be even more emphatic, it does not even exist. It is not present. There is no evidence of a limited separate self. When that is seen, when you truly recognize this point, what happens is that this knocks the belief out of the whole structure. So you have a look and realized there is no separate "I." I am not a deficient separate "I." I am not a person. I am not an entity like that at all. If someone comes along and says, "Poor John is not enlightened" then who is that referring to? Once that central lynch pin is questioned, all possible self-centered thoughts are invalidated. The point "Sailor" Bob made to me was that when you see that the "I" is not present, then all of your suffering, seeking, doubts and problems are resolved. There is a cause and effect to it. The central "I" thought is the cause, and the other beliefs and concepts depend on that. So without the cause, can there be any effects? This was the point he made.

This brings it all back home for us. Assuming we understand what is being pointed out, then the question is—have we seen for ourselves that the separate self is not present? I certainly did not see it at first. If the mind throws up these identifications, such as "I am this, I am that" and they are given reality or belief and taken as real, then in spite of whatever theoretical understanding we have, we still have not seen that the "I" is an invalid reference point. What was strange for me was that I had been quite familiar with Ramana Maharshi's teachings. I was very aware of his teaching of "self enquiry," which was an analysis of the mind to see if the root "I"-thought, as he called it, was there or not. He talked about this a lot and it seemed to form the cornerstone of much of his teaching. So when people approached him and said they were not yet free, he kept saying things like, "Well, who are you talking about? Have a look? What is that 'I' that is in bondage?" So I had heard something along these lines, but it was not clear to me what was actually being advised. I had met several Western teachers who were trying to present Ramana's teachings, although they had never met him. That was a red flag in itself. Looking back, I see their understanding of this was very unclear and confusing. As a result they have never really helped anyone as far as I can see. "Sailor" Bob was able to make this all very clear for me.

Let's try to tie it all together now. You are already totally free. There is nothing wrong with you. You already are that intrinsic reality and always will be. There is not a damn thing wrong with you. There is nothing you need to do. You can walk out this door at any time and you are never anything except that pure freedom. Your nature is simple, undeniable presence-awareness. It is not a separate person. The separate person is born in thought as a concept. Then we see that all that suffering is, is simply concepts about a fictitious self. It survives through belief. It depends upon the notion that there is a distinct separate self in our experience. That is all that is happening. Then you take a step back and realize that it is all a conceptual construct based on an erroneous view, a mistaken idea. What gets pointed out is that there is no evidence that you stand as a separate being apart from present awareness. You cannot find a separate "I" in the picture at all.

No matter how hard you look, no matter where you look, no matter how much you explore and examine, if you try to trace back and locate this seemingly separate self, there is no evidence for it. You will never find it. You cannot find it. There is nothing there. To see this takes the belief out of the whole conceptual structure. There is nothing theoretical about it. It is not even a practice. It is not something that is "maybe, maybe not." It is a very clearly experienced thing, just as clear as if you thought that there was a snake on the table and then you looked and realized there is no snake here. There is nothing theoretical about that. You would no longer be suffering under that belief.

So we need to have a look and examine to see where is this "I" that is the root of all our troubles. What I like to say is that suffering has a cause, but when you search for the cause you find that it does not exist! In the recognition that the cause is non-existent the trouble of suffering is resolved. So once we have heard all of this, we can embrace this and recognize the truth of it for ourselves. There is nothing difficult about it once we get the essentials clarified. There is no need to wait around for years, practicing, waiting, hoping, doing this, doing that. In all of that you can easily miss the root of it. And the results of this understanding are immediately evident. When suffering arises in our experience, it is now recognized as thoughts. They are clearly seen to be about a separate self. Right out of the gate, you are able to recognize and appreciate that the very root of the mechanism is not valid. Is there any evidence of a separate self? If so where is it? Did you ever find it? All these things are there for you to see for yourself.

At one point it just dawned on me. I thought, "Here I am present and aware. There is no doubt about it." "There is no way I am separate from that awareness." I could see that as clear as day. I would see some thoughts, feelings and perceptions go through. That is all that I could see. I was looking at all this and thinking to myself, "So, where is the separate self?

Where is John Wheeler, the entity, the one who has all the problems and doubts? I see thoughts come and go, but I do not see any evidence that those thoughts are who I am. It is the same with the feelings and sensations." As you look in your direct experience, all that you see are some thoughts, feelings and sensations going through. So this person that we have taken ourselves to be is not really present in direct experience. It is only an assumption. The mind has created this notion, but there is nothing to substantiate it. We cannot discover any particular thing that is the separate self. You could say that the thought "I" is present as a thought. But that is a thought. It is not who you are. You are the awareness that knows that thought. The thought comes and goes. Even if you are not thinking that thought, you are perfectly fine.

These are the things that become clear. Nisargadatta Maharaj once said, "All suffering is based on the belief in a person, and there is no person." And that is the essence of it! That is what was pointed out to me, and I found it was enough. You do not need anything more. To see the truth of who you are and dispel the illusion of what you are not is more than enough. My years of seeking, searching, suffering, feeling limited, assuming I was a defective person—all that just ended. And as we sit here right now, all there is, is this presence of awareness. There may be a few things appearing in that, but none of it is separate from awareness. The root of all suffering is the notion that I stand apart from the intrinsic awareness. That belief in separation feels limited. It creates a sense of being incomplete. It fuels the search to define what that assumed person might be. But come back to present experience, and you will see that you have never been a separate being. You are being itself. You have never stood apart. Therefore, the basis of all the conceptual suffering is just simply invalid.

To view things from this perspective basically takes care of the root of the problem. What can happen then? All that can possibly ever happen to you is that the mind can generate residual habits from the past. They used to come up a lot, so they might resurface in the mind. But they do not touch awareness. They do not knock you out of what you are. They do not refer to a real person because there is nobody there. They are just like husks or lifeless things that show up on the screen, but they are no longer believed. They float through and leave you as you are. They do not mean anything about you. They are just a mechanical, residual effect, like a spinning potter's wheel once the power is shut off. It is just an impersonal happening. And chances are that, because there is less and less belief in them, they will resolve and take care of themselves. They will be less and less present to worry about. People sometimes feel that only when thought activity stops happening and they do not have any self-centered concepts coming up, that they will be free. Well, that is falling back into another self-centered story! The thoughts are impersonal. They do not even belong to awareness. They belong to an image of an entity that died along the way because it is not real. Who we thought we were is like an old, dead dream with no substance.

After I met "Sailor" Bob, I was thinking, "When am I going to get wrapped up in the seeking and doubts again? When are the problems going to come back? It cannot be this simple!" Yet I actually found that everything was perfectly resolved. I did not need to work on it, perfect it, go back to "Sailor" Bob for a tune up or anything like that. He just laid it all out on the table. I never heard it so clearly from anybody. A lot of teachings hint about self-knowledge and the truth of who we are, but then they push you right back into the practices, the techniques, the gurus, the future attainments and so on. So they have got you back in the mind again, thinking you are not yet whole and complete. "Sailor" Bob was one of the few that would say, "This is what it is. There is nothing else!" Or he used to say, "There is nothing beyond 'no thing.'" You see this for yourself and you are basically done with it. You are not going to get a practice or a promise of enlightenment in the future. Who needs that when you already are what you are seeking? I can say with full confidence that this way of looking was absolutely able to resolve all my remaining doubts. There is no doubt about it!

Things like karma or rebirth—all the traditional, doctrinal concepts—are still in reference to the imagined entity. The clear view of things knocks out the interest in a lot of that stuff. If you think, "I have still got to do this. I have to do that"—well, that only applies if you are a separate "I." If you are pure awareness, which is intrinsically free by nature, then you do not have any need to do anything at all. Who is there to do anything if there is no person present? So all of the spiritual concepts come tumbling down. It is all based on speaking to the assumed entity. In Tibetan Buddhism it is said that Buddha's highest and most profound teaching was a direct pointing to our innate nature of intrinsic awareness. But if people did not embrace this view, then Buddha gave out various relative teachings. Why? To address the conceptual position that people imagined themselves to be in. But the highest teachings say very clearly that those relative teachings are incapable of yielding lasting freedom. The reason is that they are all based on a false premise. They are only given as a stepping stone for someone who is totally committed to the idea that they are some kind of entity. But those relative doctrines are not the highest teaching. They are not the central teaching. They are not capable of revealing our innate and ever-present freedom. For that, you must relinquish all concepts, paths and approaches and see that here and now you are free, because you have never for a moment been anything other than that pure presence-awareness itself.

## Further Titles from Non-Duality Press

*What's Wrong with Right Now?*, 'Sailor' Bob Adamson
*Presence-Awareness,*'Sailor' Bob Adamson
*Awakening to the Dream,* Leo Hartong
*From Self to Self,* Leo Hartong
*Already Awake,* Nathan Gill
*Being: the bottom line,* Nathan Gill
*Awakening to the Natural State,* John Wheeler
*Shining in Plain View,* John Wheeler
*Right Here, Right Now,* John Wheeler
*This is Unimaginable & Unavoidable,* Guy Smith
*Perfect Brilliant Stillness,* David Carse
*Oneness,* John Greven
*I Hope You Die Soon,* Richard Sylvester
*Awake in the Heartland,* Joan Tollifson
*Be Who You Are,* Jean Klein
*Who Am I?,* Jean Klein
*I Am,* Jean Klein
*Beyond Knowledge,* Jean Klein
*Living Truth,* Jean Klein
*Life Without a Center,* Jeff Foster

Printed in the United States
153601LV00003BA/10/A